YOUTH SUICIDE

A Comprehensive Manual for
Prevention and Intervention

BARBARA BARRETT HICKS

National Educational Service
Bloomington, Indiana 1990

Edited by Larry W. Barber, Ph.D.
Director of the Center on Evaluation, Development and Research
Phi Delta Kappa
Bloomington, Indiana

Cover design by Tim Mayer

Printed in the United States of America

Printed on recycled paper

ISBN 1-879639-10-6

Table of Contents

PART ONE: PREVENTION

PART TWO: INTERVENTION

PART THREE: POSTVENTION

ACKNOWLEDGMENTS

The author would like to express appreciation to all who worked to plan and implement the comprehensive network of support for youth who may be at-risk of suicide which is defined in this book. Their dedication to developing a community/school partnership never wavered, and their strategic plan has become a reality.

The author is also appreciative of the response of the youth to this network of support and to their acceptance of the fact that the adults of the community really do care. Additionally, the author is grateful that youth are learning to trust the adults around them, and their peers, to be helpful when they are having trouble coping with their world.

Special appreciation is expressed to Rev. William Keagle, who from the beginning shared the dream of giving youth other options to their suicidal intentions, to Michael Bach for his expertise, to Merlin Outcalt for his special perspective, and to my husband Wes, for his patience. The author is also appreciative of the support and encouragement freely offered by my sons, Scott and Mark.

Preface

Suicide of youth is an increasing reality in our society, usually premeditated and, in most instances, preventable. This book describes a systematic and comprehensive community approach to such a prevention effort. The approach described is one which any community can adopt to create and implement a youth suicide prevention, intervention and postvention program. Such a program, a community–school partnership, is fundamental in preventing youth suicide (Hamlin, 1982).

The process of program organization, described in this book, involves all crucial components of the community concerned for youth. Such key components include community leaders; law enforcement personnel; hospitals; mental health clinicians; clergy; school administrators, faculty and staff; parents; youth-serving agencies and organizations; media; and the youth themselves. The described organizational process is strategically planned; supported from the top down in all components; and includes mechanisms for awareness, education and action.

While the focus of the book is on preventing youth suicide, many other benefits are derived when a community mobilizes to develop such a program. Examples are strengthened referral and treatment options for at-risk youth, an increased understanding of the needs of youth in general, an enhanced self-esteem for youth who experience the caring and support of the community, and a strengthened sense of community, mobilized in a common cause. Additionally, the feeling of panic which surrounds the issue of youth suicide is replaced by a sense of unity and productive concern for youth at risk of self-harm.

Many individuals must play a crucial role as a community organizes to address youth suicide. The top-down strategy of program development defined in this book places a primary responsibility on local officials, such as the mayor. Community leaders must openly reflect the view that a focused and united community effort can prevent youth suicides. In addition to contributing to the community awareness campaign, such leaders must also advocate for a comprehensive policy and plan, within which the prevention program can be framed. Additionally, the mayor and other leaders must clearly communicate their concern and support for at-risk youth to state legislators who, in turn, must write and enact legislation to support prevention efforts.

Other essential roles are played by law enforcement, mental health and youth-serving professionals, and by educational administrators and staff. The chief of police must provide training for all law enforcement personnel in suicide crisis intervention and postvention. School administrators must permit prevention, intervention and postvention activities within their schools, and mandate suicide prevention training for faculty, and peer intervention training for students. The mental health and youth-serving professionals and trained volunteers must co-ordinate the program development, train crisis teams in schools to intervene into suicidal crises, provide for the faculty and student training, assist schools to develop postvention pre-plans and recruit and train the postvention mechanism.

It is possible to turn the tide of youth suicides. A comprehensive community prevention program, as described in this book, is a sound approach. Such a program, increasing the attention on strategies by which to identify and intervene on behalf of at-risk youth, will also serve to focus on lifting the needs of the youth of our society to the highest priority. Our youth are our future— publicly supported and strengthened resources, joint advocacy agendas for at-risk youth and broad-based coalitions on their behalf will maximize our opportunity to impact in a productive way on that future.

BARBARA BARRETT HICKS

Introduction

Suicide is the most rapidly growing cause of death among youth between the ages of fifteen and twenty-four—and it is the most preventable (Cantor, 1987).

There are few greater human tragedies than that of a youth taking his own life. Most of us have great difficulty in thinking about or talking about suicide. When we do, it is usually within the context of our adult pressures, responsibilities and stresses. We acknowledge that adults may have problems coping with these pressures but find great difficulty understanding that children and teens are considering suicide in ever-increasing, epidemic numbers due to pressures in their lives.

 Studies show that half of all American adolescents seriously consider suicide by the time they graduate from high school. One in ten actually plans his or her own death, and every minute a young person attempts suicide—an estimated total of more than 500,000 attempts every year. Between 1955 and 1975, the numbers of youths who completed suicide in the United States rose by 300%.

Suicide of youth is a reality. It is usually not impulsive, however, but is most often premeditated. It may be done on impulse, true, but it is a decision that is usually given long consideration. It is possible, then, for the observant adult and peer to spot a potential suicide—if one knows what to look for, what to "listen" for.

Research on this problem points to a variety of solutions. This book addresses one: the creation of a community/school prevention network of caring and concern.

Depression which can lead to teen suicide knows no economic, religious or family boundaries. Teen suicides occur within strong and caring families as well as dysfunctional ones. It is crucial for parents, as well as educators, to become aware of the great

9

potential to enter into a cycle of avoidance which can prevent the recognition of signs of depression and suicide in any teen. Parents, communities and educators, therefore, must prepare to prevent and intervene into youth suicidal behavior with education and with awareness.

Educators, parents, community mental health professionals, staff of youth-serving agencies and youth themselves must be armed with the tools to intervene into a suicidal crisis. The system thus created, teaching adults and peers to identify the potential youth at-risk of suicide, is a key factor in preventing that death. The consensus is growing that our society can no longer ignore the rising tide of youth suicides and that the community, in partnership with the schools, should take the lead in prevention efforts.

This book was written to assist communities and schools to develop a comprehensive network of support for youth at-risk of suicide. This responsibility is too large for any one component of a community. It is, however, a task which can result in a successful prevention effort if planned and implemented as a co-ordinated program involving all key components of the community concerned for youth.

As each community develops a network of awareness, education and action—a network of educators, parents and youth—this network will translate into a system of caring and responsiveness for at-risk youth. This system of support will communicate understanding and concern and be a comprehensive and effective preventive mechanism.

PART ONE

Prevention

CHAPTER 1

Prevention Process

PROGRAM RATIONALE AND PURPOSE

Almost one-quarter of all adolescent deaths are from suicide (Harkavy Friedman, et al., 1987). The absolute frequency and varying forms of suicide or self-destructive behaviors in this age group are not statistically known, but studies suggest that a variety of forms of suicidal behaviors are relatively frequent, with over 60% of samples of adolescents studied reporting having suicidal thoughts. Of particular concern in one study by Harkavy Friedman, et al. (1987) were the findings that almost 9% of the high school students studied reported having made a suicide attempt. Also reported was that over half of that group made at least two attempts.

Suicide attempts among adolescents are occurring more frequently (Gispert, et al., 1985), and at younger ages. Suicide is reported to be the third leading cause of death in the United States for the adolescent population of fifteen to nineteen years of age (National Center for Health Statistics, 1978), in spite of the fact that it is probably significantly under-reported (Dublin, 1963). The suicide rate among children ten to fourteen years of age has more than doubled, and, for the adolescent population in the United States, the rate has tripled in the last twenty years, especially for white males.

Suicide is not a bizarre and incomprehensible act of self-destruction (Shneidman, 1987). Rather, suicidal youth use a logic and a style of thinking which brings them to the conclusion that death is the only solution to the problems which they are facing. This unique style can be readily seen, and there are steps we can take to stop suicide if we know where to look.

Shneidman (1987) states that "suicide is not random; it never

13

occurs pointlessly or without purpose" (p. 58). It is a way out of a problem, a crisis, an unbearable situation. It seems to be the only available answer to the question: "How do I get out of this?"

All youth have a need for security, achievement, trust and friendship. These needs form much of the landscape of their inner lives. The aim of suicide is to stop a painful existence. Shame, guilt, loss of effectiveness, frustrated dependency and other feelings have all been proposed as real causes of suicide. But underlying all of these is a sense of powerlessness and impotence. The suicidal youth feels that no one can help with this pain and there is nothing to do except commit suicide.

An at-risk youth reaches the point of suicide out of the pain of not having these inner needs met adequately. If an intervenor can discover the location of the pain and lessen the level of suffering, even just a little, suicidal youth will choose to live, not die.

Youth suicide prevention has a focus which is more comprehensive than that of preventing actual death by suicide. The successful program will not be a "quick fix" approach. Some communities may have both the expertise and the resources to develop and implement comprehensive programs, others may need initially to utilize outside consultants to help them develop the best program for that environment in the most efficient and cost-effective manner.

Comprehensive suicide prevention programs incorporate each of the three major components of prevention, intervention and postvention. A program utilizing crisis intervention techniques for youth in a community-based setting has been shown to be viable and valuable in the identification and resolution of problems of individual youth and, specifically, problems of youth at-risk of suicide (Sawicki, 1988).

Dealing with crises experienced by youth, including suicidal crises, requires an approach that is different from traditional models of therapeutic intervention. Preventive intervention which involves immediacy of response and optimal flexibility is required in working with at-risk youth. The results of such community-based intervention strategies — integral to the community program model described in this book — indicate that the youth for whom an intervention has occurred shows signs of reduced conflict in a shorter period of time and a greater willingness to become involved in more traditional supportive and/or therapeutic services.

A primary goal for a suicide prevention program is the development of a process for identifying students at risk for self-harm. Thus, a successful program should include the following minimum components:

- Training for parents, teachers, and other school personnel to identify students at risk.
- A suicide prevention curriculum taught to students to prepare them to identify suicidal behaviors in their peers. This material should be taught by qualified educators, counselors or community resource persons.
- Training for school psychologists, social workers, counselors, nurses and other key school staff in crisis intervention.
- A community network established to provide support services and awareness to the community at large, to parents, clergy and human-services personnel. This community network is also the foundation for a postvention mechanism as a preventive for a "cluster" suicide event.

Fortunately, the youth suicide rate in any given school or community is low. This fact makes it difficult to measure the effectiveness of a program in reducing the number of attempted and completed suicides. Effective measures include:

- Data on what students learn from the peer curriculum.
- Attitude changes toward suicide, and the willingness to intervene if a friend appears suicidal.
- Increases in referrals, including self-referrals, of youth at-risk to school personnel and to community resources.
- Educator, parent and student reactions to the suicide prevention efforts.

and will assist in an evaluation of the program impact.

It is said that the youth of today have no place in American society—not in our homes, not in our schools, not in society at large. Our youth have a premature adulthood thrust upon them, and they are expected to confront life's challenges with maturity and with little preparation.

Our youth are, however, our next generation and the future leaders of our nation. Their need is real and pressing. To develop effective prevention programs for our youth is a critical priority.

Community co-operative planning will result in the gift of assuring our youth that they *do* have an important place in our society, both as our young people and as the leaders of our future (Vidal, 1986).

Scope of Problem

Adolescence is considered by some adults as a carefree time when typical teenagers have a car, money to spend, friends and few adult responsibilities. Additionally, suicide has been considered throughout history as a mysterious act and as an unacceptable or taboo behavior. As a result of both of these considerations, suicide statistics for the adolescent age group have been practically unattainable.

The rise in adolescent suicide, however, has been so dramatic since the 1960s that it can no longer be ignored. The most recent information indicates that at least five teens in the United States commit suicide daily. These data become even more frightening when we remember that the trend to cover up this "unacceptable" behavior still exists and that many suicides are disguised as accidents, murders or simply unexplainable deaths. Youths suicide in small towns, in large cities and on farms. Boys and girls are equally at-risk, but boys are four to five times more successful due to the more lethal methods which they choose for their suicide attempts.

Contrary to any rosy, trouble-free picture of youth, adolescence is, for many of our teens, the most "roller-coaster" time of life. This period of growth, mentally, physically, emotionally and socially, is characterized by rapid changes. For many youths, it is a time when too many changes are taking place too rapidly for some to cope.

Many adults fail to realize the problems of adolescence, and this causes a great deal of alienation among young people. To many adolescents overwhelmed with adult experiences, decisions and consequences for the first time, suicide seems to offer the only way out. The majority of these youth are, however, ambivalent about suicide. The majority of those who attempt suicide do not really want to die.

Generally, one of the common stresses of adolescence preceeds youth suicidal deaths. Such stresses are experienced every day by countless teens who do not respond with suicidal behavior. Thus, to explain suicide, we need to look beyond the precipitating stressors to those factors which diminish coping abilities, which seem to remove coping options or which have decreased supportive mechanisms in the life of that youth (Shaffer, 1987).

Often a teen who commits suicide does so very shortly, perhaps within hours, after finding out that they are facing difficulty — with grades, with their family, with plans for their future, or with a peer relationship — when they are afraid and uncertain about the consequences. There appear to be relatively few cases of suicide in which no immediate precipitating stress can be identified and in which evidence of longstanding life-coping difficulties is also lacking.

The characteristics of youth at-risk of suicide will be discussed at another point in this book. It is important, however, to note now that it is believed that the greatest single deterrent to youth suicidal behavior is the presence of supportive, caring and courageous parents, educators and peers. These supportive persons who simply "tune in" to the youth who is overwhelmed with a problem or who is not coping well with the process of living in our society are the key to youth suicide prevention.

CURRENT RESEARCH PROGRAMS

There is a proliferation of research being conducted in this country in an effort to compile data about the youth who may be at-risk of suicide and about the recently identified phenomenon of "clustering" or "copy cat" suicide among youth. Such research is critical as we seek answers to this epidemic and to the composition of the most effective preventive programs to address this issue.

One goal of such research is to enable the enactment of legislation which will assist communities to implement effective and cost-effective prevention programs. One mandate of such legislation will be to train educators, parents, peers and significant others to identify and thus to successfully deter youth who may be suicidal.

Important studies are being conducted currently at the Rush–Presbyterian–St. Luke's Medical Center in Chicago (Clark, 1987). The efforts of this project are to expand what is already known about youth who suicide—and of the role of substance abuse, depression, age, grieving and the media on that phenomenon. This research is being conducted in order that the necessary prevention programs of the future can be constructed from a solid research base.

The Rush–Presbyterian–St. Luke's study is a Psychological Autopsy Study of Completed Suicide in Adolescents. The families of youth who suicide in the Chicago area are extensively interviewed. Researchers then reconstruct the psychological and psychiatric state of the youths who suicide in the weeks leading up to the suicide.

Some key emerging data is important as it addresses the issue of substance abuse and suicidal risk. New research clearly is suggesting that youth who are hospitalized for major mood disorders, such as depressive illness, and who have a history of *both* alcohol and drug abuse, are at the greatest risk for suicide. These findings indicate that, while treatment appreciably lowers the suicide risk in youth who struggle with depression alone, when substance abuse is also present, that condition needs to be treated vigorously to reduce the risk of suicide.

Legal Issues

As communities and schools begin to address the need to develop youth suicide prevention programs, they need to consider and understand concerns for legal issues and potential litigation in such program efforts. It is important to place this issue in a position of proper understanding in order that the program be developed to meet the needs of youth without undue concern for litigation.

The most general interpretation is that the risk of malpractice is far greater if schools and communities do not provide the help needed for youth at-risk. Since malpractice is a possibility when dealing with suicidal persons, however, it is prudent to be aware of basic precautions when involved in preventive programming. Each locality and each state may have varying laws which are somewhat different from those described in this book. The following basic legal considerations and precautions are offered only as a guide for placing this concern in proper perspective. It would be wise for each community to explore with counsel what differences might exist from those considerations which follow.

Basic Legal Considerations and Precautions

1. *Suicide must be proven.* Legally, suicide is presumed not to have occurred as an essential premise of life. When doubtful or equivocal suicides are at issue, a psychological autopsy is often done to determine the actual cause of death. This is an extensive reassessment of the events preceding and surrounding the death, with all factors taken into account. Extensive interviews are conducted with persons who knew or were closely associated with the victim for at least six months prior to the death.

2. *Proximate cause must exist.* In legal terms, *proximate* cause and *remote* cause are elements for evaluation in ascertaining negligence or malpractice. Proximate cause means that, due to a clear error of omission or commission on the part of the professional, volunteer or faculty member, the victim was so influenced that suicide followed. Without such influence, suicide would not have occurred. Remote cause is that which exerts some influence on the subject but which is not so directly impactful that death would ensue. Remote cause is insufficient for proof of malpractice; proximate cause is necessary for conviction.

3. *The Average Man or Person Standard enters.* This standard states that the professional or volunteer intervenor behaved in a manner, at all times, consonant with what would be expected and provided by another person with equal training under the same conditions at that particular time. In essence, the suicide prevention intervenor would do well to constantly ask if what is being done is likely to be the same thing that another would do under those circumstances.

4. *Never delay or avoid consultation.* No intervenor can do everything under all conditions. Be ready to ask for assistance or suggestions from another responsible party. If a legal action should follow, the intervenor is better off demonstrating that a single opinion or judgment was not all that entered into decision-making or disposition of the case.

If these considerations are observed, those involved in the implementation of a youth suicide prevention program should have little fear of being found culpable in litigation which may surround a suicidal death. In fact, as previously indicated, there is far more concern for litigation if a community and school neglect to plan and implement effective prevention programs. Most would agree that it is negligent to *not* teach faculty to identify at-risk youth, to *not* offer support to high-risk students or to *not* intervene into suicidal behaviors.

Youth at risk of suicide are of critical concern today. It is important to understand the legal parameters of dealing with such youth, but far more important to place concerns for legal issues in their proper place and assertively move ahead with prevention programs for such youth.

CHAPTER 2

Program Development

Creating a new program within a community is accomplished through a process known as community organization. Organizing, as it is discussed here, is a painstaking, hard process. However, it produces sound results. A primary reason for community organization is to give power to persons who do not have it—power, in this instance, to advocate on behalf of youth at risk of suicide, to create networks of support in the community for all youth, and to assist youth through the problems of adolescence to an adulthood in which coping skills are adequate.

PLANNING PROCESS

Community organization is a process with one main goal—change within the community and schools on behalf of youth. This process involves initially four phases as interested persons work to establish a prevention effort for youth at risk of suicide. These phases are:

I. Become Familiar with the Community
II. Learn about the Issue: Arouse Interest
III. Establish a Decision-Making Task Force
IV. Program Development/Implementation

Except for the sequence of the phases within the process of organizing, and the process itself, there are no hard and fast rules that cannot be altered to conform to the needs of your particular community and situation.

In Phase I, as organizers, you should become familiar with your community and your youth in ways you probably have never before considered. Learn about the rate of youth suicide attempts in your community. Learn about the attitude of educators,

21

educational administrators, clergy and the community at large toward the topic of youth suicide. You may discover barriers which need to be resolved as well as resources and strengths upon which to build your program.

Learn who the decision-makers are — what is the social structure and the economy of the community. Find out where the resources are to which youth who are at-risk can be referred. Define your community and create a profile of the youth within that community. It is during this phase that you will begin the important task of creating a community awareness regarding your concern for youth and for the subject of youth who may suicide. Begin to develop your "pitch" about what you have learned about your community and what you want to change about it.

During Phase II, you will begin to use your knowledge about your community and the youth in that community to begin to talk about the issue of youth suicide and to arouse interest in the need to address this issue in a systematic and comprehensive manner. You will begin to develop a sense of how the youth suicide prevention program in your community might look, where it might be located, and what the components of that program might be.

In Phase III, your primary task is to create a Task Force on Youth Suicide Prevention. The composition of this group is critical to the success of your program development efforts. This task force should be viewed as a permanent advisory group which gives the strength and power that is needed by your prevention program.

The task force is selected to represent all major components of the community which might be concerned for youth at risk of suicide. The members should include educators, educational administrators, human-service clinicians, parents, clergy, law enforcement personnel and selected youth. This group will become the central authority for the direction of a comprehensive program.

The task force, providing a variety of perspectives, will be the key to a program for youth suicide prevention which can work within your community and within your schools. It provides a critical forum for understanding and for decisions which involve many community sectors on behalf of youth. Thus, it is important that the task force membership include persons who make primary decisions regarding youth services as well as visible, concerned and influential persons.

The fourth phase is both exciting and dangerous. This is the process during which the program components are determined and set into place within the community and schools. Some critical components of this phase are leadership, communication and evaluation.

The leadership of your program must be identified. This leadership will need to be an effective spokesperson, one who will speak for your program, not just his/her own personal beliefs. This leadership will need to observe the program development, to evaluate the decision-making processes, to lobby for the need to proceed according to a plan, and to exercise the power base which has been created within the task force.

Accurate and continual communication is critical. Community education is a part of this communication function. The task force must educate the public as well as continue the education process for the membership of the task force.

Evaluation of each level of program development activities and of the program components must begin early and be a continuous process.

COMMUNITY AWARENESS ACTIVITIES

The prevention model discussed in this book represents components of a community program established to address the issue of youth suicide. The total program is designed to be developed over a five-year period of time. The phases of this program design are:

    I. Community Awareness
   II. Community Education
  III. Community Intervention Linkages
  IV. Community Crisis/Postvention

It is strongly recommended that any community effort to address the issue of youth suicide incorporate all of these components. To plan to do otherwise is to develop a program which may be fragmented and primarily crisis-responsive. This results in a mechanism which makes the statement to youth that they are liable to receive the most attention from the community when they are experiencing a crisis. This is a dangerous message and does not assist youth to be better able to cope with the stressors of their daily lives.

The model described in this book identifies the first year of program development as devoted solely to community awareness activities. Activities of community awareness are intertwined with the process of organizing your community and developing your prevention program.

Citizens in the community need to hear the term "youth suicide." Youth and adults need to lose their apprehension toward talking about this concern—need to begin to discuss the issue and to ask questions. In this process, it is possible to dispel myths about youth suicide and enable people to begin to deal with some of their own personal feelings which surround this topic.

The media can be very helpful, particularly if you can organize print and radio media around network television airings of programs regarding youth suicide. It is important to develop a trusting relationship with journalists and television personalities. This trust will respect the need of the media to report the news but will emphasize the need to treat this subject with sensitivity and with professionalism. During this year of community awareness activities, you will be able to initiate a dialogue with both print and electronic media about the indicators which are accumulating to show the critical role of the media in the clustering phenomenon. This evidence, and suggestions for the development of guidelines for your area media, are discussed in detail in Chapter 4 of this book.

The program's second phase, Community Education, is planned to be the focus for the second year of program development. This builds upon the Community Awareness efforts and becomes educational in nature. Specific curriculum outlines are designed and used to teach targeted groups throughout the community about youth suicide (see the Appendix for examples).

After the curriculum is written, volunteers are trained to use it. They are asked to present only the material in the curriculum to insure that the information shared across the community is consistent, correct and objective. It is believed important that personal experience, emotionalism and unpredictability are danger-ous strategies and that conformity to a curriculum offers a more secure forum within which to discuss youth suicide.

Groups targeted to be educated are service clubs, church groups, parent groups and governmental bodies. This effort creates a solid base of support within the community. This solid support base will eventually prove to be a critical component when the efforts begin to concentrate within the schools, with educators and with the youth themselves. This base of support, with the media and across the community, also makes the management of post-vention activities following youth suicides a more rational and objective process, and one which can effectively prevent an extensive clustering event.

Access to the School Environment

The process of accessing the school environment needs to be carefully planned. An underlying premise is that all activities conducted within the school environment, with faculty, with students and with postvention efforts, are done only by invitation from the school and as a guest within that environment. This is important, to enable the administration of the school district and of each individual school facility to maintain control over these activities and over the events which they might precipitate. This insures that the school environment will assume responsibility for events which might surround or follow educational, prevention, intervention or postvention activities.

A key factor in achieving this access is open and complete communication with all levels of the school administration. A strategy which is recommended is to meet with all of the superintendents of all school districts within which activities will be conducted, to explain those activities and to receive their concerns. This also is a time to assure them that they will maintain control over those activities and that they and the principal have the option to deny access to their districts or buildings. Experience has shown, however, that, given the opportunity to express their reservations and to understand that the educational and prevention activities will be carefully structured and controlled, these administrators are very open to youth suicide prevention efforts within the schools.

Following the meeting with the superintendents, their tacit approval of the program development enables a similar meeting with the principals of all schools within which preventive efforts will be conducted. The principals are given the same assurances and opportunity to express concerns and reservations. As you can assure them that their superintendents have approved the activities,

our experience is that they will not often offer resistance to prevention activities within their school. If they do, however, this must
be respected. Again, our experience has been that, if a principal
might be hesitant, the eventual discussions among his or her peers,
which reflects satisfaction with the prevention program efforts in
other schools, will be a key factor in changing that hesitancy to a
welcome.

   This process now frees the faculty and staff members within
each school building to co-operate fully with prevention program
efforts. The support which has been created across all levels of the
community and within all levels of the school administration gives
security and comfort to educators and youth as you now proceed to
teach prevention techniques.

CHAPTER 3

Characteristics of the Suicidal Adolescent

Teenagers of today generally are experiencing more stress in their lives than at any previous time. The rapidly changing society of today has placed the teens in a position in which they are expected to confront the challenges of life with maturity and with little time for preparation. The adults of this generation are many times too busy with their own pressures to be helpful to the youth (Elkind, 1985).

Contemporary American society has thus struck youth in general a severe blow, rendering them more vulnerable to stress while exposing them to new and more powerful stresses than ever faced by youth before.

For most teens, however, this time of adolescence, though difficult, is a time successfully navigated. They emerge with a sufficient and clearly defined value system, with adequate coping mechanisms and adequate self-esteem to become successful adults. All are fragile during this time of adolescence, and some are at increased risk of suicidal behavior. Research studies now in progress are beginning to provide provisional data which describe these at-risk youth.

MYTHS ABOUT ADOLESCENT SUICIDE

It is important to discuss and dispel common myths which abound regarding suicidal youth and youth suicide. Myths prevent youth and adults alike from dealing with this issue in a proper and preventive manner. Some of the more common myths include the following misconceptions.

Myth: Adolescence is a carefree time of life. As adults think of adolescence as a happy time during which the youth has few adult responsibilities, suicide by one of these carefree youths is regarded by parents as a personal failure (Ray & Johnson, 1983). This results in denial of a youth being at-risk and in hiding a suicidal death as "accidental." The overwhelming guilt which surrounds such an event, and confusion for peers of the youth who died, results in long-term problems for friends and family alike. A danger in this situation is that peers of the youth who died — peers who may also be at great risk of suicide — are not recognized as being at-risk.

Myth: Those people who talk about committing suicide never do (Allen, 1987). The most tragically misinterpreted statement of all regarding suicide victims, including adolescents, is that as long as one threatens suicide there is no danger of follow-through. Hyde and Forsyth (1978) note that studies indicate as many as 60% of persons who commit suicide have made some definite prior statement as to their intent. Any verbal threat is a cry for help. Suicide threats may shift to attempts in a matter of minutes (Miller, 1975). According to Giovacchini (1981), the reason troubled youths talk about suicide is because they are desperately hoping for someone mature and concerned to intervene before it is too late. Because of the unpredictable outcome, no threat should be taken lightly.

Myth: A suicidal "type" of person exists. Persons often have a misconception that suicide is common only to those youth who are "rich" or "poor" or that suicide "runs in the family," etc. Suicide knows no class or distinction. All kinds of youth end their own lives regardless of age, sex, race, economic background, mental or physical state (Klagsbrun, 1976). Prior suicide or suicidal behavior of a family member, however, can increase the likelihood of children becoming suicidal. This is due in all likelihood, not to familial tendency or genetics, but to modeling the behavior of the suicidal relative (Coleman, et al., 1984).

Myth: Suicidal youth are fully intent on dying. Most suicidal youth are undecided about living or dying, and they "gamble with death," leaving it to others to save them (Schneidman, 1985).

Myth: Once a youth is suicidal, he is suicidal forever. Most individuals who wish to kill themselves are suicidal only for a limited period of time. If they can be supported during this crisis, they will rarely become suicidal again (Mcguire, 1984).

Myth: Improvement following a suicidal crisis means that the suicidal risk is over. If a youth who has been depressed or suicidal seems to be coping better and is in a better mood, what may really have occurred is that a plan for suicide has been developed and decided upon. This fact may make the person seem improved, but he or she is in fact at greater risk than before. The concerned person must explore with that youth the reasons why he/she seems better. Most suicides occur within about three months following the beginning of "improvement," when the individual has the energy to put his/her morbid thoughts and feelings into effect (Ross & Lee, undated).

Myth: All suicidal youths are mentally ill. Studies of hundreds of genuine suicide notes indicate that, although the suicidal person is extremely unhappy, that youth is probably not mentally ill (Schneidman, 1987).

There are many other myths surrounding suicide, but these are the most common and the most important to dispel. Suicidal youth are youth who are having difficulty coping, are asking for help and who, for the most part, can be saved by caring, concerned and informed persons.

YOUTH WHO ARE AT-RISK

Characteristics of the suicide-prone youth are so complex and numerous that their description could easily be the subject of an entire manual. However, data which was recently summarized from the New York State Psychiatric Institute Project, a still-unfinished project, offers provisional statements about at-risk youth (Shaffer, 1987).

• "About one-third of teenage suicide victims are known to have made a previous suicide attempt" (Shaffer, p. 611).

• Moreover, one-third abuse drugs and alcohol.

• Approximately half of at-risk teens experience intense mood changes and aggressive outbursts. This behavior may coexist with periods of depression.

• Uncomplicated depression, without any associated behavior problems, is uncommon. Miller (1975) indicated that the most common emotion felt by suicidal persons is depression. The depressed adolescent, however, almost always keeps the depression concealed.

• A subgroup exists of teen suicide victims who have not

previously appeared to be suicidal. But such teens have worried a great deal about getting things "just right." They may have been excessively anxious before tests and unreasonably upset at times of change and on moving to a new home or school (Shaffer, 1987).

• As the incidence of teens who experience manic-depressive or schizophrenic psychosis is very low, only a small proportion of all teen suicides occurs in this group. Among teens who are psychotic, however, the rate of suicide is extremely high (Shaffer, 1987).

• Biochemical abnormalities consisting of low levels of serotonin have been consistently identified among suicidal, aggressive or impulsive teens (Shaffer, 1987).

• Suicide is familial—but it is not known if this is due to modeling of behavior of another family member or due to a genetic factor. Evidence is accumulating to show that imitation may be an important facilitator of suicidal behavior among youth.

The adolescent years are difficult for many youth, with changes so great that they cannot be dealt with rationally by some. Thus, careful observation of youth for the above characteristics—"tuning in" to how they act and to what they say—can assure that effective prevention efforts are focused on those youth who are in danger of suicidal behavior (Nelson, 1981).

WARNING SIGNS OF SUICIDE

Some warning signs of youth who are at-risk of suicide are quite obvious, while others are subtle and difficult for even the experienced professional to detect.

Thus, it is important to remember this advice: while 95% of suicidal youth are ambivalent about dying—do not really want to die—5% are intent upon self-destruction. The persons who implement prevention and intervention strategies, therefore, must not feel that they "have to play God." If a youth completes a suicide in spite of your efforts—you must believe that you have done your best!

The warning signs of youth who are suicidal can be categorized into four broad areas: verbal, behavioral, situational and syndromatic (Morgan, 1981). Thus, the following discussion describes the behavior patterns and signs to observe in potentially self-destructive youth as they fit into these four areas.

Verbal Signs

Verbal signs, often overlooked or dismissed, are probably the most evident and obvious clues. They include actual direct statements concerning death wishes or suicide and indirect statements which may be reflective of potential suicidal intentions. Direct statements are often a true statement on the part of the speaker. They include comments such as:

"I wish I were dead."
"I don't want to go on living."
"I'm going to kill myself."

Indirect statements may include language such as:

"How do you leave your body to science?"
"Why is there such unhappiness in life?"
"Thanks for everything you have been to me."
"I won't be around much longer to bother you."
"You won't have to worry about me any more."
"Thanks, you don't know how much you have meant to me."

Both direct and indirect statements should be treated very seriously by family, educators and peers. The youth making such statements should be questioned directly by a caring adult or peer about the reasons why he or she has said such things. Youth tend to give honest answers when confronted by someone who really cares about their welfare.

Behavioral Signs

According to Ray and Johnson (1981), the most serious sign of a youth at-risk of suicide is an unsuccessful suicide attempt. No attempt, no matter how seemingly weak or ineffective, should be ignored for what it was. Some troubled youth may make weak attempts to gain attention, but this attempt can turn to a more lethal method if ignored (Klagsbrun, 1976).

Another behavioral sign that a youth is planning to take his or her own life is the unexplained "setting one's affairs in order." This may include the youth giving away prized possessions such as a stereo, jewelry, a pet, etc. This is interpreted by some as actions which place these prized possessions in the care of someone who will care for them as has the suicidal youth. These actions can signal impending death.

Other behavioral changes which need assessment include marked and sudden changes in attitude and behavior. Any erratic behavior seeming to have no rational explanation should be considered a warning sign of suicidal intent. Some behavior changes may include excessive irritability, complaining of small annoyances, inability to concentrate, crying, difficulty making decisions and excessive guilt (Den Houter, 1981).

Situational Signs

Family strife in which a youth is involved is among the most important incidents which can provide indicators that a youth may be at risk of suicide. For the fragile adolescent, the loss of a parent, alienation from family or problems brought on by any sudden change within the nuclear family may set the stage for youth suicide (Morgan, 1981).

A youth may also view a loss of job, loss of love object, and so on, as threatening to life and, due to his/her inability to cope with these situations, choose suicide. These situations are certainly not always responsible for a suicidal death but may serve as clues to potential suicide victims.

Syndromatic Signs

Although not a factor in the majority of youth suicides (Glaser, 1981), the most prevalent syndrome of suicide remains that of depression. Because of the prominence of depression in some suicides, it is important to recognize the clues or characteristics of depressed young people. The symptoms of depression include:

- Sleep disturbances
- Loss of or increase in appetite
- Feelings of hopelessness, low esteem and despair
- Excessive fatigue or lack of energy

- Abrupt behavior changes
- A feeling of a sense of isolation

These symptoms are considered to be more serious if their intensity, duration and/or combination is greater than normally expected in that individual or in the normal adolescent.

Some also include "risk-taking" behaviors and defiance, or the desire to control their own destiny, including death, as other syndromes which can be warning signs of a youth at-risk of suicide.

ASSESSING SUICIDAL RISK

Suicide is not a spontaneous activity but is usually the result of a long-term, gradual wearing-away process called suicidal erosion (Miller, 1984). What is eroded is the ability of the youth to cope with anger, stress, loss, frustration, disappointment, etc. Usually, this erosion takes place over many years, but even the adolescent suicide victim probably experiences a suicidal erosion taking place over a shorter period of time. Adolescents are known to kill themselves impulsively, but such a youth does not instantaneously transform from a non-suicidal person into a highly suicidal individual from one moment to the next.

If a youth experiences a sudden ending of a romance or a failing grade, that event may be the *precipitating* event, but it is not the *cause* of that suicide. There is never a single cause of a suicide — usually multiple causes.

As indicated previously, as most youth who are at-risk of suicide are ambivalent about dying and actually hope to be rescued, about 75% will give clear notice of their suicidal intentions in the form of early-warning signs. A suicidal youth who gives such warning signs will present more than one. Therefore, only one warning sign in isolation should not result in a panic reaction on the part of the observer. The observer should look for a clustering of warning signs (Friedrich, Reams & Jacobs, 1982).

Once you become suspicious about the possibility that a youth is at-risk of suicide, the best procedure is to quickly approach that youth in a warm, accepting, non-judgmental manner. It is imperative to directly ask a question such as: "Have you been thinking about harming yourself?"

Do not be hesitant to ask this question. Most youth will give an honest answer. You will not plant the idea of suicide in the mind of someone who has not already thought of it on his or her own. To hesitate based on this belief is a tragic mistake.

Your question may lead to an expression of emotion by that youth, but it will not create a crisis which does not already exist for that youth.

If the youth admits being at-risk, it is imperative that you assess the degree of risk immediately. It is also critical that you do not leave that youth alone until you have deemed him/her to be not at-risk or until he/she is supported by another concerned and responsible person.

To determine the degree of risk, you will need to learn the answers to specific questions in the correct order. Always begin your assessment by asking, *"How would you harm yourself?"* The answer to this question will indicate to you if the youth has a plan for suicide formulated. Following the determination that a plan is in mind, Miller (1984) offers the acronym S–L–A–P to assist with this assessment process. Obtaining answers to the questions of this acronym will indicate the level of suicidal risk for the youth of concern.

S = *How "Specific" is the plan of attack?* The more specific the details which can be related, the higher the degree of present risk.

L = *How "Lethal" is the proposed method?* How quickly could the person die if the plan is implemented? *The greater the level of lethality, the greater the risk.*

A = *How "Available" is the proposed method?* If the implement to be used is readily available, the level of suicidal risk is greater.

P = *What is the "Proximity" of helping resources?* Generally, the greater the distance the youth would be from helping or supporting resources if the plan were implemented, the greater is the degree of risk.

This quick method for assessing risk is not foolproof, particularly if the youth also abuses substances or is highly impulsive. This method, however, offers a quick procedure for assessing both the degree and imminence of risk for most potentially suicidal situations.

Four additional factors which can assist you to assess the level of suicidal risk for a suspect youth are also described by Miller (1984). He suggests these factors are most helpful when the youth has made a previous suicidal attempt, but we have also found them helpful for any at-risk youth.

To assist you to remember these factors, think of the acronym D–I–R–T.

D = *Dangerous*

How dangerous was whatever was done in the previous attempt or is described in a plan by the at-risk youth? The greater the danger of that attempt or plan, the higher the current risk.

I = *Impression*

Even if the danger in the attempt or plan is not significantly high, if the individual believes or has the impression that the danger is high and will surely cause death, the present risk is still high.

R = *Rescue*

If the opportunity for rescue was great in the previous attempt or present plan, the risk is lower than if the opportunity for rescue was remote. If the chances were or are poor that rescue will occur, the present risk is high.

T = *Timing*

If the previous attempt was recent, the present risk is higher than if the previous attempt was long ago.

A determination on assessment that the youth may be at immediate risk of implementing a dangerous suicidal plan mandates that you immediately implement any process necessary to protect that youth or to provide life-saving supports. Over-reaction is always the safest course of action, rather than a more conservative course which may leave that youth free to carry out the plan for self-destruction.

Auto-Erotic Behavior

A recently emerging phenomenon which may be discovered to be a factor in what appears to be a suicidal death by hanging is important to discuss in this manual. The phenomenon involves a sexual behavior, also called "Chinese masturbation," which results in from 500 to 1,000 deaths each year which are mislabeled suicide (Bosworth, 1985).

These youths are instead victims of auto-erotic asphyxia. This is a little-known, extremely dangerous sexual practice in which the supply of oxygen to the brain is restricted, usually by a noose around the neck, as a means of supposedly heightening the pleasure of masturbation.

Although auto-erotic asphyxia has long been familiar to coroners, as well as to individuals and couples who practice sexual bondage, this behavior strikes most people as so bizarre, so shameful, that the subject is almost never discussed publicly. Parents whose sons (girls rarely practice this behavior) accidentally die during the practice of auto-erotic asphyxia generally cover up the circumstances of the death because the stigma attached to a sexually related death is greater than that attached to a death by suicide.

Some parents whose sons have died in this manner, however, are wanting to tell other parents, schools and clergy that this dangerous practice exists and to describe the warning signs of this behavior. There is no consensus, however, concerning if or how to discuss this issue with youth themselves. This book offers no advice regarding how to indicate to youth that this dangerous practice can and does result in accidental deaths.

Auto-erotic asphyxia has been defined as "self-hanging while masturbating to achieve sexual gratification" (Bosworth, 1985, p. 54). Constriction of the neck is said to result in heightened sensations which include "giddiness and light-headedness" (p. 54), according to Bosworth. Although practitioners of sexual asphyxiation take elaborate precautions in the belief that they will not endanger themselves, they do not realize that there is an extremely sensitive area around the carotid artery (the main artery in the neck, which feeds the brain). It is very easy to lose consciousness when pressure is applied to this area. The youth may do it right forty times but, on the forty-first attempt, make a wrong move and die.

Most victims seem to be happy, well-adjusted persons. Risk-taking may play a part in this behavior. Victims tend to learn of the practice from three sources: their peers, personal experimentation and pornographic literature. Victims may be found in women's clothing or with props which are indicative of sexual fantasies. Homosexuality does not seem to be disproportionately associated with this practice.

Some warning signs that a youth may be engaging in auto-erotic asphyxia include the following:

- A fascination with ropes and nooses
- The presence of pornographic literature or "fantasy props" hidden in the bedroom
- Marks on the neck which are results of a rope or noose used in the practice
- If death results, signs which are different from those of a suicidal death by hanging are:

> The victim is usually nude
> The victim is found behind locked doors
> A towel is used to protect the neck and prevent welts
> The victim leaves no suicide note
> There is evidence of sexual activity such as semen

This information is offered in the hope that the accidental deaths which result from this practice, and which are increasing the numbers of "suicidal deaths by hanging" in this country, might be prevented.

CHAPTER 4

Prevention Program Components

The prevention of youth suicide is a relatively new practice as the problem of self-destruction among the young has been growing to significant numbers only in the past twenty years (Ray & Johnson, 1983).

Research and theory on youth suicide has only just begun. Nevertheless, given the development of adequate dissemination procedures, there is currently enough information to save many lives (Allen, 1987). Effective dissemination of relevant information can be accomplished both in schools and throughout the community with planning and minimal training of volunteers or professionals.

Education is the cure for denial, stigma and mythology. Suicide of the young is a reality; talking about it prevents it. Free discussion also kills denial and opens ears and eyes to signs of suicide (Hals, 1985).

The most common prevention strategies developed for youth are school-based casefinding and educational programs. These programs, however, generally are not easy for a school district to develop in isolation. To develop a program prior to a suicidal death in the school district usually requires that the initiative for such development arises from a concerned community. The reasons for this include concerns for funding of such programs, denial that there is a need for such programs and an absence of any systematic evaluation of in-school programs generally.

As commented earlier, this book describes a comprehensive program of community and school partnership to address the concern for youth suicide.

Three basic assumptions guide such a community–school partnership:

1. An effective youth suicide awareness and prevention education program must involve all factions of a community which are concerned for the welfare of the youth in that community.

2. Such a prevention effort must involve all members of the school community — administrators, educators, parents and students.

3. The talents of the community at large, the mental health community and the school community must join into a working partnership to maximize the effectiveness of a youth suicide prevention program.

Only such a partnership, involving total community organization and networking, can provide the youth of that community with the resources which they need to avoid resorting to suicidal behavior as a means of communicating their needs.

COMMUNITY COMPONENTS

The components of a comprehensive program of suicide prevention within the community at large include awareness, education and mobilization efforts. The goals of the community activities are to:

- Create an urgency within the community for addressing the needs of youth who are at-risk of suicidal behavior
- Develop a common language regarding this issue with which common strategies may be developed
- Create an understanding of the need to develop programs of prevention, which include:
    Teaching about childhood depression
    Information about therapeutic resources in the community
    Assisting parents to be more competent in parenting children and adolescents
    Implementing *Life Planning and Coping Skills* curricula
    Enabling the schools to develop funding resources with which to establish school-based program efforts

A way to initiate the development of a strong community component is to provide a community-wide seminar for professionals, educators, law enforcement, clergy and parents on the subject of "Youth Suicide Prevention." A one-day seminar is generally of great interest to the community, stimulates a common dialogue regarding the issue of youth suicide, provides a listing of interested individuals, and encourages community planning activities.

As discussed earlier, *Community Awareness* and *Community Education* are the first two phases of the development of a community-wide program. These phases provide the foundation for the prevention, intervention and postvention efforts which follow.

It is recommended that one year be devoted to *Community Awareness* activities. Important vehicles to utilize include the electronic (television and radio) and print media. The media can assist the community to discuss the problem of youth suicide as both a national and a local phenomenon. This is also a valuable opportunity to develop an attitude of trust with journalists and to help them to understand the critical responsibility of the media in presenting information about youth suicide.

Features in the media regarding youth suicide can provide an opportunity to offer factual information, to dispel myths and to begin the process of building community-wide support for youth at-risk. The topic of youth suicide is generally of such great interest that media professionals will welcome local panel discussions and editorials to accompany network offerings. This is also an opportunity to discuss youth suicide as a preventable tragedy of harsh reality and to minimize any tendency to dramatize that reality or to portray such behavior as acceptable or desirable.

Activities important to conduct concurrently with media events are informational presentations to service clubs, governmental bodies, legislators, church congregations and parent groups. It is advisable to develop a speakers bureau of persons who receive training, to be available to community groups to offer consistent information.

A thorough effort of community awareness sets the stage for the next phase of program development — *Community Education*. It is again recommended that this phase be planned and conducted over a twelve-month period of time.

If a Task Force on Youth Suicide Prevention has not been created prior to this time, it is recommended that this occur during this phase. As you begin to be more specific with information sharing and plan to develop programs within your schools, the credibility of this Task Force becomes very important to school administrators.

SCHOOL-BASED COMPONENTS

Now that you have prepared the way within the community to support the development of a youth suicide prevention program within the school setting, that school program will now be much more easily implemented and stronger. The school system will begin to recognize the concern of the community for the youth and to trust a partnership approach to the issue of youth suicide.

The schools, of all organizations involving youth, are in the most strategic position to provide a central prevention effort. Additionally, parents, community health professionals and educators themselves are becoming more assertive in asking that the schools be more involved in prevention programming (Dempsey, 1986).

Administrators and school boards raise some questions about this public pressure to implement suicide prevention programs within the schools. Some of these questions are:

• Do schools see suicide prevention programming as compatible with the demand to teach academic subjects?
• Do schools have the resources to implement such programs?
• Does the responsibility for suicide prevention rest outside the school's jurisdiction?

There are no easy answers to these questions. Yet, at the very least, schools are indirectly involved in suicide outcomes. This includes not only prevention and intervention programming but dealing with the aftermath of a suicide in a school. And, even though a school may have thus far avoided the tragedy of suicide, there is no way to predict how long it may be before such a crisis arises.

Most researchers agree that suicide prevention programming is possible for schools at a minimal cost. Inexpensive program materials are available, and community mental health professionals can help with the necessary educational activities (Grob, Klein & Elsen, 1983).

Top school administrators recognize the fact that a good program is not going to work overnight. They should not be tempted by "quick-fix" solutions, such as:

• A one-time invitation to an "expert" to address an assembly of teachers, students and parents

• An occasional suicide film or informal class discussion by untrained personnel that only serves to heighten anxieties

• Outright denial that suicide could be a possibility in our school

Such well-intentioned efforts may create the illusion that the problem is being dealt with adequately. Such solutions do not effectively deter suicide, however, and they leave a school ill-prepared to respond appropriately to at-risk youth and to survivors in the event of an actual suicide.

Thus, to avoid such pitfalls, the schools must involve community support in the planning of a comprehensive program and build that program on the foundation previously created within the community at large. This networking serves as a reminder that youth suicide is a problem, not just for the schools, but for the entire community.

A comprehensive school program begins with the fact that life for most youth centers around the school environment and that the teachers and peers within that environment are key persons to identify a youth at-risk of suicide. The counselors within the school actually have broader skills for identifying youth at-risk, but teachers are usually the first to notice problems since the classroom provides a structured setting for assessing student behavior. Thus, with adequate preparation and with support from the school counselors, teachers can become the initial agents for screening high-risk students due to this high level of teacher–student interaction (Maag & Meinhold, 1985).

Sufficient evidence exists to indicate that peer education should also be a component of a school-based program. Thus, the youth themselves are able to receive information about youth suicide and become better able to help friends who might be more vulnerable or at-risk of suicidal behavior.

The components of a comprehensive school-based suicide prevention program include an emphasis on related curriculum and materials implemented from early elementary grades through senior year at the secondary level. These components provide information for educators, parents and students. The distribution and suggested content of each component is:

Secondary School Level

1. Faculty Seminars
   Identification of At-Risk Youth
   Assessment Strategies
   Communication Skills
   Referral of Suspect Youth
2. Parent Seminars
   Similar content to Faculty information
   Parental Denial that *Their* Child Could Be At-Risk of Suicide
   Parenting the "Normal" Adolescent
3. Student–Peer Education
   Normal Adolescent Development
   Self-Evaluation of Emotional Well-Being
   Identification of a Peer At-Risk
   Assisting the At-Risk Peer to Help

Middle-School Level

1. Faculty Seminars
   Same information as Secondary Faculty
2. Parent Seminars
   Similar information as Secondary Parents
3. Student–Peer Education
   Same general information as Secondary, but with greater emphasis on personal interaction and relationships
   Life Planning Skills Curriculum Content
   Sexuality
   Stress Management
   Daily Coping Skills
   Self-Esteem and Personal Planning/Goals

Elementary School Level

1. Faculty Seminars
   Identifying the Child Who Is Depressed
   Linkages of Behavior Disorders in Children to At-Risk Behavior in Adolescents

Factors Arising during Childhood which Contribute to Adolescent Suicide
Referral of the Child of Concern
2. Parent Seminars
Parenting Skills
When to Seek Help for Your Child
Importance of Parent–School Communication
3. Student Education
Death Education
Life Planning Skills Curriculum

Do not feel a need to implement all of these components at one time. It is recommended that a strategic plan be developed by which each component can be implemented carefully and according to a predetermined schedule.

We recommend that the program implementation of each component utilize trainers who are professionals from the mental health system and community educators (who may be carefully recruited and trained volunteers) to conduct the faculty and parent seminars. Such community educators can also conduct the peer education classes and assist with the development of that curriculum.

As the program matures, it is recommended that the school system move toward greater participation by teachers and school guidance persons to conduct peer education classes for students, as well as parent seminars. Community educators can continue to conduct faculty seminars in order to relay new developments in adolescent suicide prevention and to maintain a good working relationship between the school and the community at large. The school community, therefore, gradually becomes the "owner" of the program, and "turf battles" are thus avoided and costs minimized.

Another strategy found to facilitate the successful implementation of a comprehensive prevention program at all age levels is to initiate the first program development efforts at the secondary school level. This is the local focal environment for youth suicide prevention efforts in the view of both community and schools alike. Successful implementation of efforts at this level will serve to encourage the implementation of program activities in the middle school and elementary school environments.

It is suggested that, as plans are made to broaden the prevention efforts to the middle and elementary schools, to do so as a pilot program in part of the school district or community. This will be more easily accomplished than a full effort across the entire school community environment. A successful pilot effort can then be expanded to all of the middle and elementary schools.

It is strongly recommended that some cautions be observed in the planning and implementation of seminar and classroom information to educators, students and parents. Examples of cautions are:

• Always approach any discussion or seminar presentation on the topic of youth suicide with the sensitivity that the individuals participating in the program are dealing with this topic in very personal, and at times very painful, ways. Always be alert to those persons who may not be able to remain in the session or who may need support or referral to assist them.

• Inform school administrators of the intent and progress of program development at several points along the way. This helps to develop a trusting relationship between the schools and the community as this program develops. Be certain to maintain this open relationship and never deviate from the approach and content agreed upon between the administrators and community planners.

• Develop a curriculum outline to be used for each presentation, train persons to use that curriculum outline and insist that it be followed in all presentations. This insures that the information given is consistent and helps to minimize the emotional overtones which can develop around this subject.

• Utilize a team approach to classroom content on youth suicide prevention when teaching *Peer Prevention* to students. The reasons that this is advisable are that the topic is very intense; the team can alternate presenting material and observing the students, and using a team will enable personal attention to any student who finds the topic too threatening or painful to manage.

• Try to schedule classroom presentations which are requested by a student as a class assignment as quickly as possible. Our experience is that that student generally has a very personal reason for that request and it is important to respond quickly.

• A good practice when scheduling presentations to students in classrooms when it is known that there has been an attempted suicide or other crisis within the student body is to notify the administration and counseling staff of that school of the scheduled presentation. This allows for the supportive mechanism to be alerted and ready if needed.

• Never schedule presentations to students in a school setting on the last day of the week, the last day before a holiday or the last day before a vacation. We believe it is important to allow another school day for the students to digest the content of the presentation and to seek assistance, if needed, prior to leaving the supportive environment of the school for an extended period of time.

Outlines for presentations to community groups, to educators and to students are included in the Appendix. They are only frameworks, but they can provide a consistency for your program which we believe is critical.

MEDIA GUIDELINES

Evidence is accumulating to show that imitation may be an important facilitator of suicidal behavior among youth. All who are concerned about the increasing incidence of youth suicide are critically concerned about the relatively new phenomenon of "clustering" or the occurrence of more than one youth suicide at nearly the same time or place.

Clustering can also occur in different parts of the country when a youth suicide event has been widely discussed in the media. Therefore, it is important to develop a philosophy and some guidelines by which to address this issue with both the national media resources and with your local media professionals (Robbins & Conroy, 1983).

Examples of the evidence that youth may attempt or complete suicidal acts as a result of imitation follow.

• Prominent coverage in newspapers of a suicide leads to an increase in suicidal deaths—mainly among youth—for a one- to two-week period after the news (Phillips, 1984).

• Research shows that suicide attempts and completion rates will increase during two weeks following fictional television programs which deal with teen suicide (Gould & Shaffer, 1986).

• Young attempters have had many more close contacts with others who have made a suicide attempt than have non-suicidal young people (Kreitman, Smith & Tan, 1970).

• Examples of "copycat" suicides are documented as taking place within a few hours after a fragile youth has seen a film or a news story, or read a book, featuring suicide (Shaffer, 1974).

• The occurrence of suicide clusters is believed to depend on imitation. It appears that youths who die in a cluster outbreak usually do not know one another personally but will have learned about the other teens' deaths during the extensive and/or intensive newspaper or television coverage of each case (Shaffer, 1987).

These findings are clearly relevant to youth suicide activities that involve presenting the facts about suicide to children and teens. A major challenge is to present such information in ways which will not encourage imitation. The media is a crucial arena in which great care and responsibility for this issue must be observed.

Your program will need to develop a positive and trusting relationship with your local media which will enable the media to report the news but understand the danger in irresponsible reporting around the topic of youth suicide. As you developed your Community Awareness program component, you began the process of creating a healthy exchange with the media on youth suicide. At that time, the reporters had the opportunity to hear from you your concerns and should have begun to understand their responsibility in this effort.

The majority of journalists work hard under deadline pressures, try to be accurate, have a job to do and a boss to answer to and want to be treated as decent human beings and professionals (Ring, 1984). If you accept this and are willing to believe it, you have taken the first constructive step in working with the media around the general topic of youth suicide, as well as in the event of a tragedy within your schools.

Some suggestions which are intended as guidelines and which may be helpful to you follow.

• *Deal up-front with reporters.* A good communication system with local media is essential. If improvement is needed, take the first step. Invite them to information-sharing sessions, to planning sessions, discuss the program development with them and be accessible. Be open and honest, and together you will be able to manage a crisis carefully and correctly.

• *Do not try to "stonewall" the media.* This is perceived by the reporters as attempting to stop them from doing their job. You are not their only source of information. Police reports, scanners and the coroner are other resources for reporters. You need to decide what is appropriate for the school or community to say — and say it. Prepare and issue statements or hold a briefing for the media.

If there are ground rules which you would like to have respected about interviews with students or faculty, most reporters will understand. You can be clear without being unpleasant. If you give the media something sound to report, they are much less likely to be sensational. In addition, many journalists are clearly very sensitive to the indicators that media reporting may be a factor in the clustering of youth suicides.

• *Identify a single information source.* Do this now — do not wait for a crisis. Obviously, the person selected should have good human relations skills, feel comfortable with the media, and be readily accessible. He or she also needs to know all of the facts and which ones should be shared with the media.

• *Advise school personnel of the media procedure.* Make certain that the faculty know the name and phone number of the media contact person. This enables them to defer if they are asked to comment.

We all discuss the partnership which is necessary among educators, parents and mental health professionals to effectively combat the terrible reality of youth suicide. The media can be a constructive part of that partnership as community educators, if you learn how to work with them effectively.

PART TWO

Intervention

CHAPTER 5

Intervention Process

RATIONALE AND PURPOSE

Ross (1980) and others suggest that a program developed within which professionals work with educators, trained para-professionals and non-professionals can be key in preventing youth suicides through intervention strategies. Although it is not possible to prevent every suicide, it is possible to recognize the existence of common crises that may precipitate a suicide attempt and reach out to the youth who are facing them.

Intervening into a youth suicidal crisis involves applying the principles of crisis intervention. The primary focus of this intervention is on trying to open up alternatives other than suicide, to assist the youth to regain a sense of control over his or her life. Crisis intervention, however, is only one important step in the process of working with a suicidal youth.

There are three stages at which an intervenor can be involved with suicidal behavior. These are prevention, intervention and postvention. The goal of the prevention stage is to help the youth cope with the psychological and situational stresses that may precipitate his or her suicide. Intervention consists of interrupting a suicide attempt that is imminent or in the process of occurring. The postvention stage involves following through with attempters and survivors to prevent further deaths (Battin, 1982). The most ideal stage within which to work with suicidal or potentially suicidal youth is in the prevention stage.

INTERVENTION MODEL

Interventions are focused on the current needs of the youth at-risk, resolution of the present crisis and a return to pre-crisis conditions and behavior patterns.

Specific program areas included in this intervention model are:

- Peer Intervention
- Crisis Intervention
- Preventive Intervention

The techniques emphasized here are:

- Community-Based Outreach Intervention
- Crisis Interview Techniques

There are two areas upon which intervention must be focused: the precipitating event and the youth's reaction to that event. The rule of thumb is to take any indication of suicidal thinking or behavior, reported either by the youth or by others about the youth, very seriously and to evaluate it carefully. There is little comfort in suicide death statistics (Kraft, 1980), and thus the goal of suicide intervention is to prevent a suicide through communication of concern to the youth and evaluation which determines the appropriate course of action.

Successful intervention not only resolves the suicidal crisis but helps the youth to develop alternative behavior patterns which can help keep them from developing further crises. To this end, it is important that the intervenor assist the youth to pursue further counseling or referral if needed. Crisis provides the youth with the opportunity to see therapy as a helping tool, and, if the intervention is successful, the youth will often be willing to seek further long-term treatment.

Intervention is a short-term, intensive life-saving strategy. It is a process of assisting a youth to survive a crisis of short duration and of responding to a "cry for help."

The components of a youth suicide intervention program are integrated into a comprehensive network of support, planned as a school/community partnership to reverse the rising rate of youth suicide. Intervention represents the third phase of a community program established to address the issue of youth suicide.

Youth suicide intervention activities are central components in a comprehensive program of prevention. The community awareness and education activities prepare the framework within which crisis intervention teams are prepared to function and to co-operate with the community at large. Additionally, the youth themselves must be taught how to identify their peers who may be at-risk of suicide and to intervene into a suicidal crisis when it may occur.

Community planning strategies, dealing with the media and entry to the schools are discussed elsewhere in this book. The goal of such community planning is to create a comprehensive network of support for all youth across all levels of the community and within all levels of the schools. This enables a maximally protective environment for youth who may be at-risk and require intervention support.

LEGAL ISSUES OF INTERVENTION

The program efforts which involve teaching students to implement peer intervention strategies and prepare school faculty and staff to intervene into suicidal behavior and crises are generally considered, both by the state boards of education and the courts, to be defined as "immune" activities in terms of potential for litigation.

In such program activities, which are requested and condoned by the school administration, it is important that the role of the trainer or educator from the community, the school and the student be clearly specified. The legal parameters for each role are:

• *Community trainer/educator.* The intervention trainer/educator functions within the comprehensive prevention/intervention network. Their role is that of consultant to the schools, and to the students of the schools, to provide information and to educate the school staff and students. They provide education about issues of suicide, grief and loss, postvention support and service availability following a suicidal or traumatic death. They do not function as professional counselors and do not represent themselves as providing counseling services.

• *School faculty and administration.* The school administration, upon inviting the assistance of the intervention trainer/educator, seeks the educational assistance of that person. The school remains primarily responsible for the welfare of its students while they are in school.

The legal position of school administration is that there are two basic issues involved. These are that:

1. This is an activity or program authorized by the school and performed, therefore, by persons acting as agents of that school.

2. In the event of a completed suicide following such authorized suicide prevention, intervention or postvention activities, the activity must be proven to be "willful and wanton" negligence for liability to be upheld.

If these considerations are observed, those involved in the implementation of a youth suicide intervention program should have little fear of being found culpable in litigation which may surround a suicidal death.

In fact, as previously indicated, there is far more concern for litigation if a community and school neglect to plan and implement effective prevention and intervention programs. Most would agree that it is negligent not to teach faculty to identify at-risk youth, offer support to high-risk students or intervene into suicidal behaviors.

Youth at-risk of suicide are of critical concern today. It is important to understand the legal parameters of dealing with such youth but also important to assertively move ahead with prevention and intervention programs for such youth.

CHAPTER 6

Phases in the Course of a Crisis

The goal of intervention is simply to broaden the suicidal youth's perspective — to enable the suicidal youth to change his or her focus on the plan or option of suicide to include other choices, one of those being life. This act of realizing that there is more than one choice is often the first act which results in resolution of the suicidal crisis. The suicidal youth is ambivalent about dying. Intervention turns the tide in favor of living — at least for the present.

About 80% of suicidal youth give friends and family clear clues about their intention to kill themselves. They are trying to communicate their plan and get someone to stop them. Intervention recognizes this communication and signals that someone will stop their suicide.

We can learn to spot potential suicides if we look to previous episodes of pain in the life of that youth, to the ways in which that youth manages phychological pain and for a way of coping which might be called "cut and run." This coping style is one in which the youth tends to run from problems rather than to try to solve them. Very few suicidal deaths occur without some of these previous signs.

The intervenor must ask, "Where do you hurt?" and tailor the intervention to that youth's needs. Preformulated interventions are not usually effective, as they do not fit the needs of the individual.

To completely understand any individual act of suicide, it is necessary to examine the youth, and the situation, from many perspectives, including biochemical, genetic, sociocultural and psychological. It is not the intent of this book to advocate this totally comprehensive approach but to describe the preventive steps which can and must be taken without having all the answers to our questions.

Suicidal youth do not usually give us the luxury of time to

comprehensively assess the problems. They need an immediate response to this desperate communication. An intervenor can be any prepared, caring person. This person can relieve the pain and change suicidal thinking and behavior. These interventions are much more than psychological patches. They are, in fact, life-saving strategies for suicidal youth.

A suicidal crisis is a normal reaction to a painful experience (Lindemann, 1944). Unfortunately, persons who intervene into a crisis too often do so in unstructured ways which are ineffective in resolving the crisis.

There are four phases in the course of a crisis (Caplan, 1964):

1. Initial Phase
2. Escalation Phase
3. Redefinition Phase
4. Dysfunction Phase

The youth may resolve the crisis at any phase in this continuum. Crisis, a struggle for adjustment and adaptation can provide an opportunity for growth.

INITIAL PHASE / CONFRONTATION

Crisis reactions, including a suicidal crisis, do represent a uniform and identifiable pattern that includes an acute reaction, an identified onset, and a brief period of endurance. Crisis is experienced when a youth is in a situation that is not readily mastered by previously set patterns of problem-solving.

The initial phase of a crisis is a period of time during which the youth is faced by a situation which may pose a threat to certain perceived needs. The response of the youth to feelings of increased tension is to try to utilize problem-solving strategies which previously were successful.

During crisis, there will be an increased desire to receive the assistance of an intervenor, along with an increased willingness to accept change. That is, the youth is much more open to outside intervention during a period of crisis.

SECOND PHASE / ESCALATION

The second phase of a crisis is one of escalation. If the usually successful coping measures fail and the threat persists for the youth, tensions continue to increase and anxiety and a feeling of ineffectiveness have onset. Functioning becomes disorganized, and the individual begins to resort to trial and error in efforts to master the problem.

It is helpful for the intervenor to remember that crisis refers more to the emotional state of the youth than to the precipitating circumstances. The youth will emotionally identify the crisis as an imbalance between the threatening situation and the coping resources which are available.

The susceptibility of the youth to crisis is related to his/her ability to solve problems or to utilize successful problem-solving patterns of behavior. The fewer adaptive behavioral patterns which the youth has, the greater the chance that a crisis can occur and escalate.

THIRD PHASE / REDEFINITION

As the youth continues to fail in the use of problem-solving efforts, tension and anxiety increase. The youth now attempts to redefine the problem—or may resign to failure. The youth may also, however, as a result of redefining the problem, solve that problem in a positive manner.

As a crisis is most often related to past experiences and generally involves significant other persons, such as family or peers, this redefinition can provide an opportunity for structural change within the life of the youth.

Many youth who will not seek out traditional avenues of counseling or therapy will accept the assistance of crisis intervention services. This can then, in turn, lead to referral into traditional and more long-term therapeutic support if needed, as crisis provides the youth with the opportunity to see intervention as a supportive tool.

FOURTH PHASE / DYSFUNCTION

The fourth phase, dysfunction, occurs when the problem is not either resolved or avoided. Tensions mount further for the youth, the individual passes a "breaking point" and enters a state of true crisis. At this time, a period of personality disorder ensues. The youth may now be at extremely high risk of suicidal behavior and be unable to exercise control or to avoid self-destructive impulses. The most logical course of action for intervention at this level of dysfunction becomes achieving hospitalization of that youth for psychiatric care and protection (Walter, 1980).

Suicide is usually a last, desperate cry for help. Many clues normally precede this act. Persons who are prepared to identify the signs of a youth at-risk, to recognize the phases of a suicidal crisis and to use intervention techniques can often prevent that youth from tragically ending his or her life prematurely.

CHAPTER 7

Intervention Techniques

Since the beginning of history, many cultures have chosen not to speak of self-destruction, to shroud it in silence and to deny it. In this way, the mystery and stigma which accompany a youth suicide are perpetuated. Thus, an approach which utilizes a preventive focus of candid and open discussion of suicide is now viewed as one significant aspect of both death education and of youth suicide prevention.

Educators need not fear youth suicide or opportunity for intervention into suicidal behaviors, as discussion of suicide will not make students more inclined toward suicide. The communication of facts about suicide and about intervention actually helps to modify the likelihood of an attempt (Smith, 1976).

A system of support for all youth in the school environment, as well as in the community at large, can greatly reduce the numbers of youth at-risk and those who attempt to complete a suicidal act.

COMMUNITY/SCHOOL INTERVENTION FRAMEWORK

The school system is in a unique position to provide both accurate preventive information and effective preventive intervention as part of the natural maturational process of the adolescent (Johnson, 1985). Additionally, educators have a substantial influence on the behavior of students generally, as well as in a crisis situation.

The community/school intervention model recognizes this unique role of educators but adds the strength and resources of the community as a whole to that of the educator. While the schools are the primary environment for youth, the responsibility for successful and comprehensive suicide prevention and intervention should be shared by both entities.

The intervention framework of support consists of the preparation of students, community volunteers and educators using specific curricula. The curriculum areas are:

- Peer Intervention for Students
- Intervention Strategies for Faculty
- Crisis Intervention Team Preparation in All High School Buildings
- Postvention Support Training

Educators, with experience with the program, become sufficiently informed and confident to accurately identify youth at-risk and to either directly intervene or to bring their concern to the attention of the appropriate school counselor or to an in-school crisis team member. Efforts to assess that youth, to plan the appropriate level of intervention and to notify the parents of the concern for their child begin as quickly as possible.

INTERVENTION — GENERAL STRATEGIES

Sawicki (1988) describes four factors which are crucial in successful intervention into and resolution of a crisis. These factors are:

- Immediacy of Response
- Client-Centered Delivery
- Youth Awareness of the Availability of Crisis Intervention Capability
- Flexibility

Youth suicide intervention must be immediately available and be as brief as possible in duration. An intervention response must be delivered promptly after a youth is identified as being at-risk of a suicide attempt. And, as crisis is a short-term state, most intervention goals must be accomplished relatively quickly. Sawicki (1988) describes this factor as probably the most critical of the four.

When intervention is indicated, a prepared interventionist must be ready to respond. Any delay may cause the at-risk youth to enter a higher level of anxiety, tension and helplessness. This increasing anxiety and tension will decrease the possibility of successful intervention.

Crisis intervention is most effective when provided at the time and place of crisis identification. The intervenor must meet the youth "where they are" physically and emotionally. As the intervenor enters the physical environment where the youth is experiencing the crisis, observation of that environment becomes a possible part of the assessment and intervention process. The youth is also able to perceive the intervenor as helpful in a hostile situation. This may enable the youth to view the intervenor as caring and concerned.

A school and community must widely publicize the availability of the crisis intervention resource. This publicity appears to greatly facilitate the acceptance by youth that the community is serious about preventing youth suicide. This in turn increases the chance of acceptance of intervention in crisis. Increased awareness and acceptance will enable the intervention to begin to reduce crisis precipitants more quickly. This will occur as the anxiety surrounding the intervention resource is lessened.

Persons who are prepared to provide crisis intervention must be willing to do so where and when needed. This may mean a commitment at any time of day, including evening and night hours and weekends. As youth learn to trust intervention resources, they also learn to access such resources when they face suicidal and other crises. This trust must not be violated. The price of such violation is the potential for youth to determine that those who say they care do not really care. The risk is therefore great that youth suicides will not decrease, but increase.

One way to insure that an intervenor will always be available is to structure the crisis team within each school building in such a way that someone will always be available if needed. Additionally, the crisis team mechanism within the schools can co-ordinate with resources within the mental health service system of the community at large to insure that each "cry for help" will receive a rapid and caring response.

It is important to define what is meant by the terms intervenor — or interventionist — which are used interchangeably in this book. An intervenor is not a counselor or therapist, although many counselors and therapists provide intervention.

An intervenor does not enter into an ongoing, long-term relationship with a suicidal youth, as a therapist would. Instead, the intervenor functions to keep the suicidal youth alive long enough to survive the suicidal crisis and to get him or her into a relationship with a therapist.

An intervenor is a person who can:

• Recognize the early-warning signs of suicidal risk and thus identify those youth who are potentially suicidal
• Evaluate the various risk factors which are present in the life of the at-risk youth to determine the level of risk
• Resolve the presenting suicidal crisis
• Make an effective referral to an appropriate community resource and follow up to be certain that the at-risk youth actually is linked to the resource

At this point, the intervenor removes him/herself from the suicidal situation and from the intervention relationship with that youth.

Any person who is in the emotional vicinity of a suicidal youth, including family members, educators, counselors and peers, is in a key position to act as an intervenor.

All such persons should be taught to recognize, evaluate and intervene effectively in a suicidal crisis. This means that a community/school program of youth suicide prevention must include a strategy by which all persons who are available to youth are so prepared.

The suicidal youth is trying to communicate. When persons around that youth become immobilized upon hearing a suicidal communication, they give a message of rejection and lack of caring to the suicidal youth. The communication nature of the entire suicidal action provides a major opportunity for the intervenor to help the suicidal youth.

The basic skills of intervention are active listening and empathy. As a human life is at stake, a working relationship must be established quickly in order to bring the destructive process under control for the youth.

The intervention relationship with a suicidal youth must exhibit three characteristics.

1. In the initial crisis, the intervenor must take an active role, as the youth needs to feel that something which will help is being

done. The youth needs a clear indication at this point that there is meaning to his or her life.

2. The intervenor needs to assume an authoritarian role with a suicidal youth. The intervenor must temporarily be in charge of directing the youth until he or she can assume self-responsibility.

3. The intervenor should involve helpful, significant others in the intervention. These people, who are significant in the life of the at-risk youth, can be instrumental in helping to build up the youth's feelings of self-worth and self-confidence.

The manner of the intervenor must be confident and patient. An essential part of this patience involves a sense of timing. The intervenor must show that he or she cares, and this takes time. A co-operative trust is a goal of intervention.

The intervenor needs to really listen to the youth—listen in a non-judgmental manner—really hear the message—and make appropriate responses. The goal is to move the youth toward being more able to handle his or her own affairs.

It is important to remember that a suicidal crisis is most often of short duration. Helping the youth through the crisis will most often save that life.

Maintain contact with the youth until the crisis is resolved— and, if the contact is by telephone, work to obtain as much specific information as possible regarding where that youth is located and what he or she is experiencing.

Remember:

- Do not express shock over anything you are told.
- Do not debate with the youth.
- Never try to physically remove a weapon from a suicidal youth. Remove the weapon with talk and manipulation. Never risk your own life.

Remember that, even though the youth may display definite improvement after the crisis is resolved, that youth must be carefully watched for a while. There is great danger of suicide following apparent improvement. This occurs as the youth has gained sufficient strength to commit the act of suicide, may have decided upon a complete plan for suicide, and has made the decision to commit the act.

Grezegorek (1979) has termed this phenomenon the "light bulb" suicide. He applies this term as it is analogous to a light bulb that glows very brightly toward the end — then suddenly burns out.

CRISIS INTERVIEW

A tool which may be helpful for the intervenor to use in working to resolve a suicidal or assaultive crisis is the crisis interview (Hersh, 1985). This model, while it appears complex, is not, and it provides a good framework for facilitating the expression and cognitive understanding of painful affect. The crisis interview concept can be used by anyone who acts as an intervenor.

The goals of the crisis interview as described by Hersh are:

- To re-establish psychological equilibrium
- To ensure that the youth's judgment is intact so that the youth is no longer a danger to him/herself or to others

Five steps are defined in the crisis interview. Although a certain logical order for each step is apparent, the intervenor does not need to follow a sequential pattern.

Each step is briefly outlined:

Step 1: *Approaching the Situation*

The intervenor needs:

Calm confidence. Your manner indicates that you are there to help.

Hopeful expectation. Your manner reflects that, "Together we will work this out."

Space, time and attention. Minimize time pressures and other distractions. Talk in an area where interruptions are minimal and which seems safe.

Step 2: *Making Contact*

The intervenor needs:

Empathy. Be open to share the burden of the experience. This may require some courage in the face of deviant behavior.

Non-verbal body language may be as important as the words you use.

Authenticity. The at-risk youth will be very alert to the genuineness of what you say and do. If you are uncomfortable, do not hide that fact.

Activity. The at-risk youth needs to feel engaged. You must listen, ask questions and reflect feelings. Keep the youth focused. You do not, however, have to both be talking continuously.

Directness. Getting to the point will help the youth. Do not be insensitive, but be direct.

Authority. The youth in crisis needs someone else to take charge. You must accept the responsibility for ensuring the youth's safety.

Step 3: *Making the Assessment*

This step is complex, but the basic components include:

Negotiating with the youth what that youth wants to accomplish or feel (Lazare, 1976). Recognition of these desires lets the youth know that you are listening and concerned.

Gather basic information. Despite the pressure to make a rapid assessment and make quick decisions, asking the youth about school and family can help put the youth at ease and help the intervenor understand how the youth may have reached this crisis.

Mental state exam. Essentially, the intervenor wants to answer three questions:
1. How dangerous is the youth to self or to others?
2. How intact is the youth's judgment and contact with reality?
3. What was the level of functioning prior to this crisis state?

Identify the precipitating events of the crisis. The youth in crisis may have difficulty being able to fully identify precipitating events. Begin by helping him/her to identify events that immediately preceded the crisis contact. Precipitating events generally include an experience of loss—an important relationship, self-esteem or sense of mastery.

Step 4: *Making the Intervention*

As stated previously, the goals of crisis intervention are:

To re-establish pre-crisis equilibrium
To ensure the youth's safety

Essential considerations in achieving these goals through successful intervention are:

Help the youth gain an understanding of the crisis. Assist youth to a cognitive understanding of what is occurring.

Facilitate appropriate release of feelings. This facilitates equilibrium. Be prepared to experience some of the intense feelings the youth is experiencing and neither prematurely stop the release nor inappropriately extend the release of emotion.

Explore coping behaviors. Help the youth explore alternative ways of coping.

Step 5: *Making a Disposition*

This involves a review of the emotional status of the youth. If you are convinced that the youth's anxiety level is significantly reduced and that he or she is genuinely hopeful regarding the immediate future, you can discuss follow-up plans for referral. If the crisis has not sufficiently resolved, additional actions such as hospitalization may need to occur.

The safety of the youth is of primary concern. Confidentiality is not an issue if you are concerned for the life of the youth, and the youth must be told this. Consultation with colleagues or with significant others in the life of the youth is not only very important but mandatory.

Finally, it is a good practice for intervenors to meet following the crisis to debrief, to share concerns and to air their feelings.

CHAPTER 8

Intervention Mechanism Components

The best advice that we have, to prevent a single suicidal death or a cluster event, is to prepare as many caring, concerned persons as possible to intervene into youth suicidal behavior. Intervention is not a magical process but rather a demonstration of life and of hope. Intervention can be successfully accomplished by anyone near—parents, lovers, high school coaches, employers, social service agency staff and, most of all—peers.

PEER INTERVENTION

There are many indicators of a youth at-risk of suicide. A large number of these indicators point out changes in the way that that youth relates to persons around him/her, especially his/her peers or friends. One of the major signs of the depression which can contribute to suicidal feelings and beheaviors is "aloneness." The youth may isolate him/herself from friends, not taking or making phone calls or not going to the regular Friday night movie with friends. Despair and hopelessness become his companions instead.

This at-risk youth may lose interest in appearance, may become aggressive or withdraw from communication. The peer group for this youth is often the first to see these changes and to become concerned about that youth. The peers may even find themselves confronted with suicidal communications or an actual suicidal crisis or attempt.

Young people in high schools and colleges are acutely curious about the topic of suicide. Journal articles and books on the subject are often missing from libraries. Research papers and speeches are prepared and delivered by students on the subject in classes ranging from rhetoric to history. Youth want accurate information regarding suicide, especially youth suicide.

While it is acknowledged that this information should system-atically be provided to students, it is also known to be important that it should be given carefully, objectively and with sensitivity. Such information must be discussed carefully, as there is always the potential that a youth in the classroom may be dealing with personal feelings and/or experiences in—at times—very painful ways.

Education is probably the most powerful tool we have in youth suicide prevention today. Strengthening our information base and using basic caution and common sense can save our youth from suicide.

Therefore, while peers are in the most advantageous position to intervene into suicidal behaviors in their friends, it is strongly recommended that some precautions be observed in the planning and delivery of *Peer Intervention* curriculum information to students.

The approach in the model program described in this book observes the following criteria:

- The curriculum is carefully structured to include necessary facts and to avoid emotional or sensational perspectives.
- The curriculum is designed to be delivered primarily within the normal class schedule in the high schools.
- The curriculum is taught only on the invitation of a classroom teacher, a student as an assignment or other school administration and staff.
- The course content is delivered, as much as possible, by teams of two persons. This enables three adults (counting the teacher) to be present in the classroom to attend to any student who needs assistance in the event the topic is too personal or too painful.
- If possible, one member of the team should be a counselor from within the school.
- All persons who are to teach the peer intervention curriculum content should be trained to do so. This insures objectivity and consistency of delivery.
- Any student may be excused from the class if he or she wishes, but that student should be followed to determine the reason and if he/she might be depressed or at-risk of suicidal behavior.
- If a student requests the peer intervention curriculum, try to schedule that class as soon as possible. Our experience has been

that the student generally has an acute reason for making the request and may be him/herself at-risk.

• If it is known that the school or community has experienced a youth suicidal crisis recently, inform the school administration, counselors and building crisis intervention team of the request for the curriculum and the schedule for presentation. This is an important practice in the prevention of a possible cluster of attempts.

• Never schedule peer intervention classes in a school setting on the last day of the school week, the last day before a holiday or the last day before a school vacation.

In the peer intervention classes, the students are told that they are going to receive important information about suicidal youth and strategies which they can use to save the life of a suicidal friend. They are assured that the faculty in their school, including a specially prepared Crisis Intervention Team, and the presentors of the class are prepared to be helpful to them in any such intervention effort. (This means, of course, that faculty in-service seminars and seminars to prepare school crisis intervention teams have actually been conducted in your community.)

The students are told that, if they are concerned about a friend who may be suicidal, they must act in a mature, assertive manner as they intervene into that suicidal event for their friend. They are also told that the presentors have confidence that they would be able to respond in such a manner.

They are informed that no one expects them to try to "play God" but to use the information which they are receiving to truly be a friend. The reward is to probably save the life of that friend.

It is important to stress:

• Never attempt to physically disarm a suicidal person.

• Some suicidal persons are going to die no matter what we do. We must just do our best to prevent that suicide from happening.

• They should stay with the suicidal youth until someone else can take over.

• *Get help.*

• Confidentiality "goes out the window" when you are concerned that a friend may harm him/herself.

- Suicidal behavior is a cry for help—an extreme communication—*so communicate.*
- If you are concerned for a friend, be persistent until you can get a parent, a teacher, a counselor or a minister convinced of your concern and willing to see that your friend gets help.

A friend who cares enough to enter the frightening world of a youth who is suicidal will receive the greatest gift—a friend who is alive.

CRISIS INTERVENTION TEAMS

The task of Phase III (Community Intervention) of the comprehensive youth suicide program is to develop and link services throughout the community into a strong intervention network for suicidal adolescents. One of the goals of this phase is to create a crisis intervention team.

The team in each school building is identified by the building administration or principal. The administration is asked to make a commitment to the team members who are identified that they will be allowed the time to attend the required crisis intervention training seminars. Additionally, the administration is asked to guarantee their support to the team members, as they will work in the event of a student crisis which might occur within the school environment.

The strategy used to obtain such commitment from the administration of the high schools is to meet with them as a group. The agenda for that meeting includes a discussion with the principals of the need for the crisis intervention capability within their schools and a request that they co-operate fully with that crisis capability in its development and utilization.

The crisis intervention team concept is explained as one component of the community/school partnership, which includes:

- Community Awareness Activities
- Faculty Education
- Peer Intervention for Students
- Postvention Support Mechanism
- Suicide Survivor Support Groups

It is hoped that administrators reflect complete acceptance of the concept. Additionally, they should make the commitment to assist with the identification and preparation of their building team and provide support for that team, as it is they who will work to manage a crisis.

The only criteria asked for the team members is that they be:

- Faculty or staff who can easily establish a rapport with youth
- Persons who feel that they can function well with a team in a crisis event, provided that they are prepared by seminar to do so

Each administrator is asked to identify a team which will range in size from three to five individuals. The number depends upon the size of the high school.

The training for the crisis team members is conducted in two two-hour-long workshops. The topic areas include:

- Current Research about Youth Suicide
- Youth Suicide Statistical Data/Incidence
- Theories Regarding the Rapidly Increasing Youth Suicide Rate
- Mal-adaptive Coping in Adolescents
- Intervention Team Concept
- Crisis Team Role in an Academic Setting
- Suicide: Developmental Emotional Escalation
- Temperament Types: Adolescent
- Warning Signs of Adolescent Suicidal Behavior
- Crisis Intervention: How to Manage
- Networking Within Each School
- Networking Within the Community at Large

Each building team is given the charge to return to their home high school environments to form supportive and informed networks there. Such supportive networks will function in the event of students in crisis giving strength to the efforts of student peers and faculty alike in such crises.

This crisis intervention team mechanism must be revitalized at least every two years. In the model described in this book, a responsible agency such as the schools or a mental health agency should assume the initiative to see that this is scheduled and conducted. At the time of revitalization, the school administrators will be asked to update their crisis team member appointments to fill any slots which result from faculty or staff leaving or no longer wishing to serve as a crisis team member. Additionally, the responsible agency should plan for the training seminars to be repeated and for updated information to be shared with the intervention team members. A bonus at this time is the opportunity for any teams to share with the larger group any actual crisis events which they may have been asked to handle in their school environments. This lends an atmosphere of "do-ability" to the training which these teams receive.

As the preventive continuum strengthens within your community, if resources permit, it is a good idea to prepare teams within each middle school as well. Our experience has been that this younger population is at increasingly higher risk each year.

Another strategy which can strengthen the networking capability community-wide is to include your postvention volunteers in the seminars which prepare your in-school crisis intervention teams. This provides an opportunity for sharing of theoretical and practical information and for valuable networking which will greatly facilitate these two groups working together if postvention support is ever needed.

INTERVENTION FOLLOW-UP

While it is true that most youth suicidal crises are short-term events and are not likely to be repeated, it is also true that the suicidal state was a clear communication of a youth having severe problems. Therefore, the community/school mechanism must include strategies for follow-up after the crisis is resolved.

The preparation for such a follow-up mechanism begins in the very first stages of the comprehensive community program development. The process begins with learning about the strengths and weaknesses of your community, of discovering resources and gaps in services for youth and of learning where the power and the barriers lie with regard to meeting the needs of your youth. Out of this information base can come the development of a comprehensive directory of youth services and resources in your community.

Any directory information must be regularly updated and made known to those who will deal with youth in crisis or who will be in a position to consult with those intervenors. Such a directory is fundamental to a sound referral system for youth.

A primary goal of crisis intervention is to move the youth through the suicidal crisis and to a therapeutic, helping resource, or combination of resources, which will work to stabilize that youth and will assist that youth to adopt better coping abilities. Thus, a key follow-up activity is referral.

It is important to utilize the referral mechanism normally in use within the school. This will facilitate better ongoing support for that youth within the school setting.

The decision to refer a student for individual evaluation, counseling or other support must be made in co-operation with, or by, the administration or counselor from within the school setting. This could be a member of the crisis intervention team which is in place in that school. The referral of youth should be a fluid process involving all persons who are significant to that youth.

Preliminary to any strong referral system is a program of information exchange to assure that all—educators and administrators, school counselors and intervention teams, direct-service mental health professionals, clergy, trained postventionists, parents and youth—understand the ethical, professional and legal parameters within which all must function. This foundation provides clear understandings of both the potential for assistance and limitations of all resources.

In the actual referral process for an individual youth, it is necessary to assist that youth to make some determinations of what assistance would be both necessary and/or perceived as helpful. A question which can be asked which will help in this determination is: *"Who do you feel would be most helpful to you now?"*

The answer might indicate a parent, teacher, counselor, clergy or a peer who could be asked to assist in supporting that youth initially. A response indicating that *no one* would be helpful (indicating a feeling of isolation) would mean that *you* need to continue to support that youth until a clinical counselor or therapist can provide an evaluation of that indication of feeling of isolation.

Sharing of pertinent information about the youth and about the crisis event is an important component of the referral process. Sufficient information must be shared to enable planning how resources should be utilized for that youth.

In addition to the youth who has experienced the crisis event, the youth who is not able to adequately resolve his or her grief response to a youth suicide or other tragedy may require referral. Evaluation of this student will assist you to know what level of support is needed.

Examples of levels of support are:

• *Educational/information sharing* in a group, class or assembly (assemblies are not a preferred method) or via a school newspaper.
• *Grief resolution education* in a group setting.
• *Grief resolution* in one-on-one discussion with a crisis team member or other significant person determined by questions to ascertain who that person might be.
• Referral to a *school counselor* or other faculty or support staff such as the nurse, principal or coach. At times, the referral agent may be able to facilitate a dialogue between a student and a school counselor not normally assigned to that student but with whom the student has indicated a feeling of comfort and trust.
• Referral to *outpatient counseling* in the community. This resource will depend on various factors, including confidentiality, financial reality, trust and availability. Community resources which may be appropriate include clergy, community health center staff, professionals in private practice (including social workers, clinical psychologists and psychiatrists) and counselors available in youth-serving agencies.

In addition to determing *what* resource is most appropriate, you will also need to determine *how* a referral will be most successful. It may be necessary for you to:

• Go with the youth to a counselor
• Make an appointment for that youth with the consent and approval of the youth
• Simply give the necessary information to the youth to enable him or her to go to the counselor
• Involve the parents to enable them to facilitate a referral for their youth
• Call an ambulance to have a youth transported to emergency care

Do not hesitate to ask for assistance or to make a referral. Call upon whomever is needed, depending on the severity of the situation. Do not try to handle everything alone.

Convey an attitude of firmness, hope and self-assurance so that the students will feel that you know what you are doing. They will then also feel that you will do whatever is necessary and appropriate to help them.

Educational leaders like to believe that they are prepared for every possible situation and/or crisis. Seldom, however, are they ever prepared for managing a situation in which a space shuttle explodes while students watch, for telling students of the death of a classmate or for helping students in a suicidal crisis.

Thus, it is critical for a community and school system to co-operate fully in creating a network of support. Both entities must share the responsibility to be responsive to youth in crisis and must assist each other to "be there" for all youth. Such a mechanism as this is mandatory in this era if we are to help youth to cope with their stresses and pressures. And, as we clearly communicate to those youth that life is an exciting challenge and one that we will meet together with them, they will learn to trust the world around them.

We have the power to prevent all but a tiny percentage of youth suicides. The work which will prevent these tragedies is work which will make our future generations stronger. All such effort is deserving of our best.

PART THREE

Postvention

CHAPTER 9

Postvention Process

This section of the book is a guide to communities to assist them to develop a supportive mechanism available to schools following a youth suicide. This model represents the only known mechanism which, it is believed, can prevent a cluster event, according to a report from the Centers for Disease Control (O'Carroll, 1987). Others, such as Dr. Willie T. Hamlin (1982) of the Department of Child Psychiatry, Howard University Hospital, also perceive the prevention of cluster suicidal events as a problem which must be shared by the community working with the school environment.

According to O'Carroll (1987), although scientists have not quantified the benefits of various suicide prevention approaches, there is compelling evidence that suicides can trigger more suicides, and community agencies—public and mental health agencies, schools, government, police and the news media—should cooperate in advance on a community plan. Such a plan, defined in this book, is entitled a Postvention Plan.

MISSION STATEMENT AND PURPOSE

The mission of the postvention network is to deal with the aftermath of a youth suicide in such a manner as to prevent further suicides among youth.

When one youth dies by suicide, the impact is felt throughout the school attended, the entire school district and the entire community. It is important to be prepared to deal openly with all youth who may be affected either directly or indirectly. The situation which places a survivor of suicide at greatest risk is that which does not allow for appropriate expression of the feelings surrounding the death (Stevenson & Powers, 1987).

It is important to systematically plan for how the survivors of a youth suicide will be helped to deal with their guilt, their grief and anger. The population of primary concern for the effort is usually the student body and the faculty of the school attended by the suicide victim. At times, the postvention effort will have to extend to elementary or middle schools, where younger siblings of the victim attend, and to other middle or high schools, where peers of the victim attend (Valente & Sellers, 1986).

A postvention network of support is *community involvement* to deal with the tragedy of youth suicide. Trained adult volunteers organize to form a support team to assist school personnel — to open discussion, encourage communication and expression of feelings and to defuse the crisis surrounding a youth suicide.

It is not the function nor the intent of postvention to do any type of psychological counseling to individuals. Postvention team members work with school faculty and staff to help students to deal with their shock and grief through facilitation of discussion and with understanding support. Students who are identified as needing individual counseling or referral are given assistance to access those services through the referral procedures of the school.

Key Points

- The postvention network is established to assist the schools to deal with the aftermath of a youth suicide.
- The goal of postvention is to prevent youth suicide "clusters."
- A postvention network is comprised of volunteers from the community who are trained to assist students and faculty to express feelings in open and appropriate ways.

POSTVENTION MODEL

This postvention model represents the fourth phase of a community program established to address the issue of youth suicide. Basic to the success of all four phases of this program is the work of a Task Force on Youth Suicide, which has been appointed prior to any program development. This task force, chosen to represent all major components of the community which might be concerned for youth at-risk of suicide, is comprised of educators, educational administrators, human-service clinicians, parents, clergy, law enforcement personnel and youth. This group is the central authority for the direction of this comprehensive postvention program.

The task of a community postvention support mechanism is to develop a responsive support mechanism for survivors of an adolescent suicide event. This is not an easy component to develop, as it is a mechanism which it is hoped will never be utilized. A postvention mechanism is a mechanism in readiness to be supportive to the schools only in the event of a youth suicide and only on the invitation of the principal of the involved school.

This model is comprised of the following components:

• Tacit approval by all high school principals and central educational administration of the school district that they will allow prevention and intervention activities to be implemented.

• Agreement by district administration and school principals that they will invite the postvention response team into their school in the event of a youth suicide.

• Crisis intervention teams identified and trained in each high school building.

• Faculty in all high school buildings who have received training sessions on identification of youth at-risk of suicide and intervention methods.

• Youth in all high school buildings who have received training on peer intervention methods.

• Community volunteers who receive training to enable them to intervene in the school environment in the event of youth suicide, as postventionists.

The primary activity of a postvention support mechanism is that of group process. Students are offered the opportunity to gather in groups of up to twelve or fourteen individuals which are facilitated by the postvention volunteers.

The usual format is for teams of two postvention volunteers to assist the group of students to discuss their feelings and to have the freedom to express their emotions. The environment is a controlled one in which appropriate expression and discussion is encouraged. It is not necessary for the group to enter into constant dialogue, and there are times when silence and quiet grief is experienced.

This environment is one in which the students can feel secure that their comments will be received in a non-judgmental manner and with confidentiality. Their questions are answered as completely and honestly as possible, and correct information is shared to dispel rumors about the suicidal death.

At times, students who have not previously known one another find the mutual support received in the postvention groups to be the basis for ongoing supportive peer relationships. In our experience, we find that some of these relationships become friendships, especially for previously somewhat isolated youth.

The postvention volunteers, providing support for communication and for the grieving process, are free to comfort the students and to provide whatever assistance is indicated, from non-judgmental listening to holding the student in their arms if that seems to be appropriate. At times, the students simply need permission to say what they feel and to behave in a manner which will help them express their shock, anger and grief.

Experience has shown that it is a good idea to display a photo of the dead youth somewhere, in order that students who may only have known the youth as they passed in the hall can know who has died and thus grieve appropriately. Students who believe that they did not know the victim, only to learn later that they *did* know that student, express feelings of anger that they were denied the opportunity to share in the grieving process.

Students may also be assisted to plan memorials to the deceased student. Care must be taken, however, that this effort does not make the suicidal death appealing or in any way desirable as a way to gain attention.

Legal Issues

A frequent issue which arises as communities begin to create programs to prevent youth suicide and suicidal clusters is that of the threat of litigation. Therefore, it is important to comment on this concern and to clarify legal parameters and roles.

The role of the postvention volunteer team member, the school and the student must be clearly specified and understood by all involved. The legal parameters for each role are:

- *Postvention volunteer.* The postvention volunteer functions within the postvention network. His/her role is that of consultant to the schools and to the students of the school to provide information, to educate the school staff and students. Postventionists provide education about issues of suicide, grief and loss, postvention service need and service availability following a suicidal or traumatic death. They do not function as professional counselors.

- *School faculty and administration.* The school administration, upon inviting the assistance of the postvention support team, seeks the educational assistance of that mechanism. The school remains primarily responsible for the welfare of its students while they are in school.

- *Students.* The student may participate voluntarily in post-vention activities. If a student appears to require further assistance beyond postvention activities, the following rules apply:
    1. The student may seek counseling with the school personnel.
    2. The student may seek counseling through public or private mental health services.

Since malpractice is a possibility when treating suicidal persons, it is prudent to be aware of basic precautions involved in such interactions. Again, each locality or different state may have laws which vary from those described in this book. Therefore, it is wise to inquire if there are differences from the precautions described here. Additionally, the same legal considerations apply as were defined in Chapter 1.

CHAPTER 10

Postvention Preparation

VOLUNTEER RECRUITMENT

The development of a postvention mechanism is difficult. The task of this mechanism is to develop a responsive support mechanism for survivors of an adolescent suicide event. The goal is to prevent the clustering phenomena which might occur following one youth suicide.

The difficulty is to create a mechanism, which it is hoped will never be utilized, a mechanism in readiness to be supportive to a school only on the invitation of the principal of that school in the event of a student suicidal death. This program component will only be utilized if other components of a youth prevention and intervention program fail. It is, therefore, a test of all previous efforts.

A postvention mechanism requires great co-operation between professional counseling practitioners, both within the community at large and within the school environment, and teams of trained community volunteers recruited from the community at large.

A dynamic, caring and responsive network of volunteers is recruited from across the community. This network can include educators and mental health clinicians as well as clergy, parents and other persons concerned for the welfare of the youth of the community. Often they are persons who have experienced a loss of a relative or peer by suicide and now are committed to preventing that tragedy for youth.

A stimulus for recruiting a sufficient number of postvention volunteers can be a seminar or workshop which focuses on the postvention process and on the need to create such a mechanism. Participants in such a seminar are asked to commit themselves to the development of a postvention network. Service clubs, churches, human-service agencies and parent organizations are other sources of potential postvention volunteers.

The persons who volunteer are asked to make a commitment to be available to function as a member of a postvention effort if the need should arise and for as long as the need exists. They also agree to participate in a mandatory postvention training program, regardless of their level of clinical expertise. This requirement is to insure that all volunteers receive the same information regarding the process of postvention function within a school setting.

VOLUNTEER TRAINING

Topics which should be mandatory training for all postvention network volunteers are:

- Theories of Youth Suicide and Suicidal Clustering
- Coping with Grief and Loss
- Team Management of the Postvention Process
- Group Process and Intervention
- Assessment of Youth at Risk
- Referral Process and Sensitivity
- Legal Parameters of Postvention

Each community is encouraged to utilize expertise in each topic area from within the professionals in that community. This facilitates the networking and communication within the community which is a critical component of any successful postvention effort.

Our experience has been that the direct-service clinical staff who will function within the postvention process should also be required to participate in the training. This is due to the unique focus of the postvention process in the educational setting. Experience has proven this strategy to be advisable, as clinicians, although well qualified to function within the postvention process, benefit from training regarding how this process is articulated in the schools. Such direct-service clinical practitioners at times have been hesitant to enter and to function within the educational setting.

The goal of training for postvention volunteers is to prepare them to act in a postvention event to:

- Open discussion with students and faculty about the suicidal death
  - Encourage communication and expression of feelings

The concern of postvention is for the emotional health of the students, their parents and the school faculty. It is *not* a function or intent of postvention to do any type of psychological counseling to individuals. The postvention team members, including clinical practitioners, are prepared to work with school personnel to facilitate discussions pertinent to the tragedy and to defuse the present crisis. The team members need to be prepared, on request, to assist with referrals of students and faculty for professional assistance which may be needed in addition to the postvention support.

A good practice is to provide continuing training sessions for the postvention team members. This provides an opportunity to update them on changes in the program protocol and for them to continue to network and become better acquainted with one another.

If actual training is not scheduled, it is a good practice to schedule opportunities for the postvention team members to meet together to share postvention experiences which have happened within the community. Actual experience with working with a student body of a school in a postvention event will serve to remove apprehension from the postvention team members and will strengthen their commitment to this need in the community.

As this postvention mechanism strengthens, some communities may find that both the schools and the postvention team members will want to work to support schools in the event of traumatic student or faculty death, in addition to student or faculty suicidal death.

Key Points

- Postvention volunteers can be recruited from all across the community and can have widely varied professional expertise.

- Postvention volunteers must agree to participate in a series of mandatory training sessions regardless of professional expertise level. This assists with the networking within the mechanism and helps to focus the postvention process on communication and support rather than counseling.
- Communities may elect to provide a postvention support mechanism to the schools for events of traumatic student death, death of faculty members, and student suicidal death.

PRE-PLANNING IN THE SCHOOLS

Once the postvention volunteers have received foundational training regarding their role in the postvention process, they should schedule planning meetings with each high school in the community to which they will be responsive. In our experience, it has also been necessary to pre-plan with each middle school as well.

This pre-planning activity is the opportunity for postvention team members to actually enter the school to which they will respond and to meet with the key administrators and staff within that building. The goal is to document how a postvention response will be conducted.

It is recommended that this activity be repeated on an annual basis to enable a smooth intrusion into the school environment by the postvention team when a crisis occurs. Current information regarding responsible school personnel, policy and procedures is important to share to minimize confusion in the event of an actual postvention.

Each school building, administration and faculty has a very different method of routine operation, and these differences become very pronounced when it is necessary to work with the postvention support mechanism after a student suicide. The pre-plan activity will provide the forum within which the school personnel and the community response persons can begin to work together and to understand how the school environment functions.

Information which it is important to share includes:

- The school administrator who will be in control in the event of a postvention support activity.
- The names and phone numbers of the primary and alternate

postvention contact persons. Home and work phone numbers are important to help assure the school administration that they will be able to quickly notify of their need for postvention support.

• The names and home phone numbers of the in-school crisis intervention team to enable early communication and rapid mobilization of support persons in the event of a student suicide.

• Rooms which will be made available for group activities.

• Policies regarding procedures for dealing with absent students considered to be at-risk and students who might wish to leave school during the school day.

Other information can be included if it is pertinent. The pre-plan will become more comprehensive each year that it is updated, and with each postvention support event.

The key benefit initially will be the dialogue and networking between the school and community personnel and the sharing of names and phone numbers of the key actors in a postvention activity.

CHAPTER 11

Postvention Protocol

There are as many different ways to plan and conduct a community/ school postvention support activity as there are interested persons, schools and communities. Additionally, any experience with a postvention support event will add other unanticipated variables to the process.

It is important to prepare and pre-plan but also to determine that the process will need to be flexible and evolving. The suicidal crisis will produce stress within both the school personnel and the community support team. Both groups must remember that this entire process is not a normal daily process and that the goal is to assist the students and faculty in the least intrusive manner possible. The needs of impacted students and faculty are of primary importance.

RATIONALE

It is important for all who interact in the postvention process to determine what role each group will ideally assume. The key groups for which a protocol needs to be articulated are the school faculty and staff, the community postvention volunteers and the persons who comprise the clinical crisis entity within the community.

There are many postvention tasks, and to clearly identify which postvention component is responsible for each is essential. Overlap of responsibility may occur, but to negotiate an interactive process which states how all are to function will avoid much confusion.

Some considerations which have been determined to be essential components of a postvention support activity are:

• The protocol which is created should provide the least intrusive support possible. This is to avoid intensifying an already abnormal situation.

- A formal procedure for notifying the postvention mechanism of the death of a student.

- A pool of available postvention support volunteers should be ready to respond if the need within the school is greater than anticipated or if support is needed elsewhere in the community.

- Tracking to other school buildings of siblings and peers of the student who has died is an important activity. It is often found that these peripheral schools are as heavily impacted as the school attended by the victim.

- The postvention support team members who begin the process in a school should make every effort to be able to continue to function with that process until the need for support is finished. This will usually continue until after the funeral for the suicide victim. This provides the students with familiar persons to whom they can relate in their grief.

- Each school day on which postvention support activities are conducted *must* conclude with a debriefing session between the postvention team members and involved faculty. This is mandated to make plans for the following school day and to insure that students or faculty considered to be at-risk or in need of support after the school day will receive such support.

- It may be appropriate to continue postvention support to youth in visitation or funeral ceremonies.

- A formal discussion of the postvention process is scheduled among key postvention volunteers, clinical crisis professionals and the faculty and administration of the impacted high school about three weeks following the suicidal death. The purpose of this meeting is to review the process, to identify weaknesses and to make recommendations which will strengthen the postvention effort.

- Contact by the postvention response team with the school should be maintained for "100 Days" following the suicidal death. This is to be certain that all students and faculty who are at-risk are receiving appropriate support.

VOLUNTEER / CLINICIAN ROLES

Due to the need for the postvention support activity to function within the academic environment, and the need to maintain an increased capability within the community to respond to youth who might be in crisis, it is essential to clarify the tasks and roles of both postvention volunteers and clinical crisis professionals.

In the event of youth suicide, or in the event of multiple youth crises occurring within a close timeframe, the crisis capability of the mental health system in a community will be severely impacted. In such an environment, many students will be referred for individual counseling, some will need to be hospitalized as being at-risk of suicide and others will need to renew previous counseling relationships to assist them to cope with the loss of their peer by suicide.

Thus, the clinician crisis professional is needed to perform those functions for which they are best prepared, to manage actual youth crises if and where they might occur. Therefore, the trained postvention volunteer can, in co-operation with the faculty within the school environment, perform the functions of postvention support, which include:

- Facilitating open communication
- Encouraging appropriate expressions of feelings
- Facilitating the grieving process
- Assisting with the identification of youth and faculty who are placed at-risk by the suicide
- Assisting the school to return to normal as smoothly as possible

The different roles and responsibilities for the postvention volunteers and community clinical crisis professionals is suggested in Appendix R of this book.

The primary responsibilities of the clinical crisis component of the postvention mechanism are:

- To receive official notification of the youth death. This formal procedure can be implemented by the coroner or the police at the time they are called to the scene of the death and certify that it has been a youth death by suicide.
- To notify the postvention team of the death.
- To identify a crisis co-ordinator to function for this postvention event to:
  - Communicate with the school postvention co-ordinator and principal
  - Mobilize the appropriate crisis staff professionals to

deal with emerging concerns with youth at-risk in the schools or community at large

• To assist with the tracking of siblings and peers to other schools than the one primarily impacted by the suicidal death.

• To communicate to postvention team members and to appropriate school personnel information about individual students or faculty who may be known to be at-risk.

The primary responsibilities of the community postvention volunteers are comprehensive. They include all of the pre-death event activities. These include:

• Conducting community awareness activities
• Designing a curriculum to be used in teaching faculty about the identification of youth at-risk and students about peer intervention strategies
• Conducting peer education classes with students
• Conducting faculty in-service programs
• Facilitating seminars to prepare in-school crisis intervention teams
• Pre-planning with all schools
• Updating school pre-plans annually
• Recruiting and training postvention volunteers
• Designing postvention event co-ordinators

The post-death event activities which are also the responsibility of the postvention volunteers include:

• Identifying the event postvention co-ordinator to the crisis co-ordinator
• Communicating with the school principal regarding how he or she wishes the postvention effort to proceed; this discussion includes:
    · How many postvention volunteers are needed
    · How and when the postvention volunteers will meet with the school faculty to discuss the postvention process
    · How the faculty and students will be notified of the suicidal death
• Mobilizing the appropriate numbers of postvention support volunteers

- Co-ordinating all postvention activities with the school administration and faculty and with the community clinical crisis component
- Performing a triage function to determine which students are in need of more than the postvention process and are at greater risk of suicide
- Conducting groups within which the students can express feelings and discuss their grief; some of this work may be conducted within normal classroom settings, particularly those classes which were attended by the suicide victim
- Assisting in communicating information regarding the need to track students to other schools and mobilizing postvention volunteers to assist with this tracking process
- Participating in the mandatory daily debriefing and planning sessions
- Supporting students in funeral activities
- Providing "100 Day" follow-up to the school

This interface of available resources and responsibilities provides a network of support to the school in response to the criteria determined by the involved principal. This leaves the key responsibility for the scope of the postvention response with the principal. It also helps to keep the process less intrusive and more perceptive of the needs of individual students and faculty. This is a support mechanism which is truly that — available to the school at the level indicated by the administration and faculty. Thus, the control for the process remains with the school.

The Role of the School

The role of the school includes maintaining primary control over the postvention process which is to occur within the impacted building. The school is responsible for the process involving the students and faculty and for referrals of students to counseling as indicated. The usual policies for student referral are followed.

The activities which are the primary responsibility of the school in the postvention process are to:

- Request postvention support
- Communicate information to the media
- Provide current listings of space available for group postvention activities
  - Plan for notification of faculty of the death
  - Plan for notification of students of the suicidal death
- Share information with the postvention network of significant or at-risk students or faculty
  - Refer students identified as at-risk of suicide
  - Provide food and respite for postvention team members
  - Conduct daily debriefing and planning sessions

The development of this or similar protocol will insure that all needed support activities are available in a timely and appropriate manner. It will also insure that confusion regarding roles will be minimized and that maximum energy can be expended to provide necessary supports to students and faculty.

The postvention process is lengthy and exhausting for those who work within it. All concerned, postvention volunteers, crisis professionals, faculty and impacted students are very tired by the time that the funeral happens. Clear understanding of the responsibilities of each component helps to conserve emotional and physical strength. This in turn assists the community to return to a more normal level of functioning.

CHAPTER 12

Peripheral Support Mechanisms

STUDENT ASSISTANCE PROGRAMS

A helpful mechanism which can greatly enhance the efforts of the community and school to develop a youth suicide prevention, intervention and postvention network is a student assistance program.

This program is modeled on the format for support of employees of a business or industry who might need treatment for substance abuse or alcoholism. The premise is to provide a confidential clinical counseling expertise from the community mental health system to the school and community environment within which youths live. The service is provided by contract from the community mental health service system with either school district or community funding. The network of counseling includes all components of the community impacting on the youth, including the law enforcement personnel (Mayo, 1984).

This counseling mechanism is supplementary to the school counselors and is more able to work within the community at large to assist youth with problems of home and society. The student assistance counselor, serving as an influence from outside the school environment, is perceived as less of a threat to confidentiality than is the school counselor. Another factor which lends strength to this approach is the automatic linkage into the community mental health care system for the student needing such linkage. The linkage with out-patient counseling capability with in-patient acute care capability, and with alternatives to incarceration in the event of arrest, make options which are positive and more viable for youth who are overwhelmed by the problems in their lives.

SUICIDE SUPPORT GROUPS

Suicide support groups are not easy to establish. They must be fostered by persons who have lost a relative or peer by suicide and who become strong enough to be able to want to offer support to others who are struggling with a similar experience. The professional or the trained postvention support volunteer can be helpful, but the impetus for this program development must come from survivors of suicide themselves (Cain, 1972).

The author of this book advocates that communities work to develop this capability to be supportive of youth having been placed at great suicidal risk due to the suicidal death of someone close to them (Hatton & Valente, 1981).

EDUCATIONAL ACTIVITIES

Educational activities which will provide an ever-strengthening community-wide base of support for and on behalf of youth at-risk of suicide include:

• Continuing Community Education and Awareness
• Regular Faculty In-Service Education programs on suicide prevention and intervention
• Continuing Curricular Information to youth regarding peer intervention and coping skills
• Death Education for Elementary Children
• Continuing Crisis Intervention Seminars for teams identified in all middle and high schools
• Parent Education to assist parents to identify problems in their teenage children and to know when and how to seek appropriate referral for counseling

All of us together can prevent youth suicide. The task will not be easy, but the most important task which we have as adults today is to help our youth to a stronger and better future.

APPENDIXES

Teen Suicide: Current Research Findings

Early (before age 14) or late (age 16 or later) onset in dating seems to present a youth with greater risk of suicide than those receiving parental consent to begin dating at age 15 years (Wright, 1982).

Alcoholism among parents seems to be a greater factor in suicidal ideation than does alcohol abuse by the youth themselves (Matter & Matter, 1984).

Birth trauma—broadly defined as complications at or before birth—is an unusual, recently proposed determinant of youth suicide. These youth may be weak and unable to cope with the stressors of life (Greenberg, 1985).

The loss of a confidant may be the most important factor, especially in "cluster suicides" (Doan & Peterson, 1984).

Clinical depression may be implicated in less than 10% of teen suicides—with impulsivity, manipulativeness and seeking revenge for perceived mistreatment by family or friends as greater determinants (Glaser, 1981).

Family mobility may create a sense of rootlessness in which the confidant may be very difficult to find (Topol & Reznikoff, 1982).

Clustering—or the self-destruction of two or more persons from the same geographic locale who are unacquainted and die at different points in time or who are friends and die on the same occasion—is a phenomenon of relatively recent vintage (Doan & Peterson, 1984).

Teen Suicide Network Model

Comprehensive Community Network Components

Phase I: *Community Awareness*
Task: To increase the level of community awareness regarding the problem of adolescent suicide and to set the stage for community network development.

Phase II: *Community Education*
Task: To educate key populations in the community about the specific needs of depressed or suicidal adolescents.

Phase III: *Community Intervention*
Task: To develop and link services throughout the community into a strong intervention network for suicidal adolescents.

Phase IV: *Community Postvention Support*
Task: To develop a responsive support mechanism for survivors of an adolescent suicide event.

Depression and Suicide: The Young Child

Teen Suicide Is a Crisis — Teens Are First Children

Preparing Children to Be Independent — A Process for Families — Educators — Communities to Share

This Concept Gives a Focus of Prevention to Educators from Kindergarten through High School

General Data

Children, even infants, are recognized as demonstrating symptoms of depression.

A frightening increase in the suicide rate is seen in very young children. Suicide is the eighth leading cause of death among children aged 5–14 years and is increasing.

Children as young as 5 years of age have killed themselves.

There are countless children who try but fail.

Why?

Emotional factors, environment and genetics are all possible contributors.

Related factors:

Environmental failure to thrive

Parental depressive illness

Loss of nurturing person

Inadequate bonding, as in:

Prematurity

Infantile illness or surgery

Placement with "strangers"

Teen parents

Suicidal Youth: How To Help

Recognize the Clues to Suicide
  Signs of hopelessness and helplessness
  Suicide threats or warnings
  Changes in behavior
  Symptoms of deep depression

Trust Your Own Judgment
  Act on your own beliefs about danger
  Do not allow others to lead you to ignore signals

Tell Others
  Share your concern with those who can help
  Do not worry about breaking a confidence

Stay with a Suicidal Person
  Do not leave the youth alone if you believe the danger is
    immediate
  Stay with the youth until help arrives or the crisis passes

Listen Intelligently
  Listen and sympathize
  Assure the youth that there are other alternatives

Urge Professional Help
  Put pressure on to seek help from a professional
  Encourage continuing with therapy even though it becomes a
    difficult process for the youth

Be Supportive
  Show that *you* care
  Help the youth to feel worthwhile again

Suicidal Crisis: How To Help

Suicidal crises usually last only a short time.

The goals of crisis intervention are:
Get the youth through the crisis without harm
Convey a sense of hope
Increase the perception of alternatives
Identify and mobilize resources

Step 1: *Assess* the suicidal risk factors
The greater the ability to describe plans of suicide, the greater
is the risk.
Step 2: *Listen.*
Really listen and hear; be empathetic.
Step 3: *Evaluate* the seriousness of the youth's feelings
It is possible for a youth to be extremely upset but not suicidal
— or to appear only mildly upset and yet be suicidal.
Step 4: Take every comment and feeling seriously
Do not discount any of the youth's concerns.
Step 5: Begin to broaden the youth's perspective of his or her past
and present situation.
Step 6: Be positive in your outlook of the future.
Step 7: Help the youth to increase his perception of alternatives to
suicide.
Step 8: *Act* to make concrete plans to resolve the problem.
Step 9: Evaluate available resources
Help the youth to identify and mobilize supportive resources
Step 10: Do not hesitate to get help.

Community Awareness Outline

I. *Presentation Purpose*
To familiarize the audience with facts about adolescent suicide in order to encourage community support for the development of a comprehensive preventive community/ school network to address concerns for youth suicide

II. *Program Format*
A. Intended audience: Service clubs, churches and governmental bodies
B. Presentation method: A lecture/discussion format supported by overhead visuals or videotape and handout materials (recommended videotape: *Young People in Crisis* [32 min.], Cantor, 1987)

III. *Presentation Content*
A. Introduce Presentors and Topic
B. Desensitize Audience to Topic of Suicide
C. Local and National Youth Suicide Statistics
D. Magnitude of Youth Suicide Problem
    Teen Suicides Reaching Epidemic Rate
    Rate of Youth Suicide Has Tripled in the Last Decade
    75% of Adolescents Have Suicidal Thoughts
    Adolescence Is a Time of Increasing Stress
    Children as Young as 7 Have Suicidal Thoughts
E. Solutions to the Problem
    Teen Suicides Can Be Prevented
    Key Factor Is an Informed, Responsive and Supportive
    Community/School Network

F. Phases in Your Community Youth Suicide Program
     Community Awareness
     Community Education
     Community Intervention Linkages
     Community Postvention Support
G. Question and Answer Opportunity

Faculty Education Outline:
Middle–Secondary Educators

I. *Presentation Purpose*
   To familiarize the audience with facts about youth suicide in a manner that leads to understanding of suicidal behavior and to encourage the participants to prepare their students for peer education information

II. *Program Format*
   A. Intended audience: Secondary and middle school faculty and staff
   B. Presentation method: A lecture/discussion format supported by overhead visuals and/or videotape and handout materials (recommended videotape: *Young People in Crisis* [32 min.], Cantor, 1987)

III. *Presentation Content*
   A. Introduce Presentor and Topic
   B. Desensitize Audience to Topic of Suicide
   C. Common Myths about Youth Suicide
   D. General Characteristics of Suicidal Youth
   E. Early Warning Signs of Suicidal Risk
   F. Assessment of Suicidal Risk
          D–I–R–T Acronym
          S–L–A–P Acronym
   G. General Intervention/Referral Strategies
   H. Question and Answer Opportunity

Student Education Outline:
Peer Intervention

I. *Presentation Purpose*

To familiarize the audience with facts about youth suicide in a manner that leads to understanding of and empathy with a suicidal peer and to encourage the participants to intervene into suicidal behavior of peers

II. *Program Format*

A. Intended audience: Secondary school students in classroom setting and groupings

B. Presentation method: Presentation by a team of two persons; a lecture/discussion format supported by a film, handout materials and opportunity for individual referral if indicated; students may choose not to participate in the program (recommended film: *But, Jack Was a Good Driver* [14 min.], CRM Films)

III. *Presentation Content*

A. Introduce Presentors (2) and Topic

B. Desensitize to the Subject of Suicide

C. Stress of Adolescents Today

D. General Characteristics of Suicidal Youth

E. Film: *But, Jack Was a Good Driver*

F. Early Warning Signs of Suicidal Risk

G. Intervention/Referral Strategies

H. Question and Answer Opportunity

Parent Education Outline

I. *Presentation Purpose*
   To familiarize the audience with facts about youth suicide and to reinforce sound parenting strategies

II. *Program Format*
   A. Intended audience: Parents of middle and secondary education level students
   B. Presentation method: A lecture/discussion format supported by overhead visuals and/or videotape and handout materials (recommended videotape: *Young People in Crisis* [32 min.], Cantor, 1987)

III. *Presentation Content*
   A. Introduce Presentor and Topic
   B. Desensitize to Topic of Suicide
   C. Early Childhood/Parent Relationships
   D. The Normal Adolescent
   E. Parenting the Adolescent
   F. Peer Pressures/Problems for Youth
   G. Indicators of Youth At-Risk of Suicide
   H. When to Seek Counseling Help
   I. Where to Seek Counseling Help
   J. Question and Answer Opportunity

Childhood Depression: Current Research

Children of parents with affective disorders are at-risk for diagnosable disorders, especially depression, and for impairment in social, behavioral and academic functioning (Weissman, 1984).

Recent advances in the understanding and assessment of depression in children have led to an increasing appreciation of its prevalence, debilitating effects and long-term consequences (Cantwell, 1983).

Non-fatal suicidal ideas and actions are common among pre-adolescents. Children can be preoccupied with suicidal thoughts for a long time and may develop distinct plans for carrying out their suicidal wishes (Pfeffer, 1987).

Childhood suicidal behavior is a complex, multidetermined symptom that involves affect regulation, early developmental experiences, constitutional factors, ego functioning and inter-personal relations (Pfeffer, 1986).

Research suggests that lifetime environmental stresses involving family changes and losses are significantly associated with child-hood suicidal behavior (Cohen-Sandler, 1982).

Childhood Depression Outline:
Elementary Educators

I. *Presentation Purpose*

To familiarize the audience with facts regarding childhood depression and linkages to identification of the youth who may be at-risk of suicide as an adolescent (Hicks, 1988)

II. *Program Format*

A. Intended audience: Elementary school faculty and staff, and pre-school teachers.

B. Presentation method: A lecture/discussion format supported by overhead visuals and handout materials

III. *Presentation Content*

A. Introduction of Presentors and Topic

B. Desensitize to Subject of Suicide

C. Encouraging Research: Teen Suicide

D. Depression and Suicide: Young Child

E. Childhood Depression: Current Research

F. Facilitating Coping in Young Children

G. Death Education

H. Local Youth Suicide Prevention Program

I. Referral of Child Depressed or At-Risk

J. Question and Answer Opportunity

Death Education: Elementary Educators

Basic premise. It is important to teach children to cope with a death experience in a manner that can assist the child to deal appropriately with grief and strong emotions surrounding a loss. Children achieve their concepts of death as they do every other concept—developmentally (Berg, 1982 and Peck, 1982).

Linkage with the issue of youth suicide. The topic of death education gains particular importance in this environment of increasing rates of youth suicide. Teaching children of the permanence of death, to grieve appropriately and to respect life is assumed to make suicide less appealing.

Concept of death for the 3-to-5-year-old child. This age is the most curious about death and is the most difficult in terms of cognitive understanding of death. This child believes that death is temporary and reversible. It is dangerous to discuss death in other than concrete terms or as glamorized. This child may want to try to join "Grandpa—who is sleeping." Allow this child to participate in ceremonies such as visitation, funeral and burial.

Concept of death for the 5-to-9-year-old-child. This age has fears of personifications of death such as ghosts and haunted houses. This age understands that death is permanent. Concepts are more easily explained to this age child.

Concept of death for the 10-year-old or older child. This child is able to cope with a realistic and mature explanation of death.

NOTE: *Some immature adolescents may not have reached this developmental level and thus are at greater risk of suicidal behavior, as they may not understand death to be permanent and irreversible.*

Children at this age should be taught:

It is normal to feel angry, sad or lonely when someone close to you dies.

It is all right to cry and talk openly about death.

Dying people and those they are leaving need to say "Goodbye" to each other.

Life is precious and should be preserved.

Death support and education activities in the event of a student death

Relate accurate information regarding the facts surrounding the death and funeral arrangements.

Explain and answer questions about the death and any causative terminal illness.

Notify parents of funeral arrangements and encourage them to take their child to funeral activities.

Allow the children time to express their emotions. Talk about the child who died and allow the children to talk about a favorite experience they shared with the deceased child.

Channel students into activities which will allow them an avenue to air their feelings. Example: Write sympathy notes to the parents of the child who has died.

Be a good listener. Pick up on the cues offered by the children.

Allow several days to return to a regular classroom routine.

Peer Intervention Outline

I. *Presentation Purpose*

To familiarize the audience with facts about youth suicide in a manner that leads to understanding of and empathy with a suicidal peer and to encourage the participants to intervene into suicidal behavior of peers

II. *Program Format*

A. Intended audience: Secondary school students in classroom setting and groupings

B. Presentation method: Presentation by a team of two persons; a lecture/discussion format supported by a film, handout materials and opportunity for individual referral if needed; students may choose not to participate in the program (recommended film: *But, Jack Was a Good Driver* [14 min.], CRM Films)

III. *Presentation Content*

A. Introduce Presentors (2) and Topic

B. Desensitize to the Subject of Suicide

C. Stress of Adolescence Today

D. General Characteristics of Suicidal Youth

E. Film: *But, Jack Was a Good Driver*

F. Early Warning Signs of Suicidal Risk

G. Intervention/Referral Strategies

H. Question and Answer Opportunity

Crisis Intervention Seminar Outline

I. *Presentation Purpose*
   To teach the audience to be able to function as crisis intervention teams in each high school in the event of suicidal or assaultive crisis in an individual school

II. *Program Format*
   A. Intended audience: Teams identified by the administration of each high school to be trained as a crisis intervention team; the team make-up may include building administrators, faculty, counselors, nurses, coaches and/or other high school support staff
   B. Presentation method: Presentation by a team of two persons within a two-hour time frame; a lecture/discussion format, supplemented by role playing and handout materials, is used

III. *Presentation Content*
   A. Introduce Topic and Presentors (2)
   B. Desensitize to Topic of Youth Suicide
   C. Youth Suicide Statistics/Current Research
   D. Youth Suicide Myths
   E. Adaptive/Mal-Adaptive Coping Grid
   F. Intervention/Crisis Team Concept
   G. Characteristics of the Typical Adolescent
   H. Adolescent Behavior Patterns
   I. Adolescent Temperament Types
   J. Characteristics of Suicidal Adolescents
   K. Warning Signs of Suicidal Intent
   L. Intervention Techniques
   M. Crisis Intervention Strategies
   N. Network Strategies/Referral Mechanisms

Crisis Interview Outline

Introduction to the model

The crisis interview model consists of five steps which can be used as a framework for dealing with suicidal and/or assaultive youth.

The crisis interview facilitates the expression and cognitive understanding of painful emotion in circumstances in which both youth in crisis and intervenors need a supportive framework in order to help both overcome the overwhelming feelings and sense of isolation inherent within the crisis event.

Goals of the crisis interview

1. To re-establish psychological equilibrium
2. To ensure that the youth's judgment is intact so as not to be dangerous to him/herself or to others

Assessing suicidal/homicidal/assaultive potential

1. The interview environment should be one-on-one in an area or room with an open door and with supportive persons and/or police nearby.
2. Use direct and non-judgmental statements.
3. Assess:
   Intensity and target of anger
   State of inner control
   Presence of intoxication
   Indications of psychosis

4. Considerations:

      Help youth focus on precipitating events
      Confidentiality does not apply
      The youth may need to be hospitalized
      Intervenors should debrief and ventilate

INTERVIEW STEP I: APPROACH THE SITUATION

Three factors to consider

1. Reflect calm confidence
2. Indicate hopeful expectation
3. Provide interaction where time pressures and distractions are minimized

INTERVIEW STEP II: MAKING CONTACT

Five facets of successful contact

1. *Empathy.* Be supportive and non-judgmental
2. *Authenticity.* Be completely honest
3. *Activity.* Listen, question and reflect
4. *Directness.* Be sensitive, but focus
5. *Authority.* Take charge, ensure safety

INTERVIEW STEP III: MAKING AN ASSESSMENT

Four facets of successful assessment

1. The process is a negotiation to elicit an answer to the question: "How do you hope I can help?"
2. Gather basic information to learn general status
3. Examine his/her mental status; answer these three questions:
      How dangerous is the youth to self or to others?
      How intact is the youth's judgment?
      What was his/her functioning level before the crisis?
4. Identify the precipitating events of the crisis.

INTERVIEW STEP IV: MAKING INTERVENTIONS

Three essential considerations in intervention

1. Help the youth gain an understanding of the crisis.
2. Facilitate an appropriate release of feelings.
3. Explore coping behavior.

INTERVIEW STEP V: MAKE A DISPOSITION

Four considerations of disposition

1. Review the youth's emotional status.
2. Can the youth describe a plan for coping?
3. Who will continue contact after the interview?
4. Is referral, hospitalization or consultation appropriate following the interview? (Hersh, 1985)

Postvention in Schools: How It Works

Postvention is a prevention model. The postvention network is established to work with students, faculty and staff in an impacted building in an effort to prevent the contagion effect of teen suicide.

When a student or staff member commits suicide, it can have profound effects on other students, faculty and staff of the school. The postvention network can help individuals deal with the aftermath of suicide.

The initial reaction to a suicide is one of shock, confusion, guilt and questioning. Due to this reaction, it is essential for a concrete plan of action to be developed. A set of guidelines and/or a postvention strategy — which is pre-planned — will assist students and faculty in dealing with the issue of suicide, the surrounding feelings and the many questions.

The goal should be a plan of action which can enable rapid and comprehensive response to support a school in the event of a suicide death. Each community, working with individual schools, should develop plans specifically to fit the needs of each school and should be enhanced by the personal styles of postvention team members and school administrators.

Postvention Network

MISSION STATEMENT

The mission of the postvention network is to deal with the aftermath of teen suicide in such a manner as to prevent further suicides among youth.

STATEMENT OF PURPOSE

Postvention is community involvement to deal with the tragedy of teenage suicide. Trained adult volunteers organize to form a support team to assist school personnel—to open discussion, encourage communication and expression of feelings and to defuse the crisis around a youth suicide.

Protocol:
Postvention Response Mechanism

Task	Community	Crisis	School
Pre-Death Event Activities			
Community Awareness	•		
Curricula Design	•		
Manual Publication	•		
Peer Intervention Education	•		
Educator In-Services	•		
Crisis (In-School) Team Preparation	•		
Pre-Plan with Schools	•		
Up-Date Pre-Plans Annually	•		
Recruit Postvention Team	•		
Train Postvention Team	•		
Designate Postvention Co-ordinators	•		
Post-Death Event Activities			
Receive Death Notification		•	
Notify Team of Death		•	
Identify Clinical Co-ordinator		•	
Identify Postvention Co-ordinator	•		
Communicate with School	•		
Request Postvention Support			•
Mobilize Postvention Team	•		
Media Communication			•
Provide List of Usable Rooms			•
Plan Faculty Notification			•
Plan Student Notification			•
Co-ordinate Postvention	•		
Perform Triage Function	•		
Conduct Postvention Groups	•		

Task	Primary Agent		
	Community	*Crisis*	*School*
Post-Death Event Activities (con'd)			
Inform Team of Significant Faculty and Students			•
Track to Other Schools	•	•	
Refer At-Risk Students			•
Provide Food and Respite for Team Members			•
Conduct Daily Debriefing and Planning Session	•		•
Intervene into Crisis or High-Risk Situation		•	
Support in Funeral Activities	•		
"100 Day" Follow-Up	•		

Postvention Network Volunteer Agreement

I, _____, agree to serve as a trained member of the Postvention Network. As an adult postvention volunteer and concerned community citizen, I agree to participate in this co-ordinated effort and to assist school personnel in the aftermath of a teenage suicide or other traumatic death. I will work to open discussion, encourage communication and expression of feelings in an effort to prevent further crisis or suicide.

As a volunteer postventionist, I agree to attend a core of training sessions and workshops as specified by the Postvention Network.

The volunteer postventionist shall adhere to the mission of the Postvention Network and shall limit his/her activities to the following responsibilities:

> The volunteer postventionist shall be available to respond immediately, upon appropriate request, in the event of a youth suicide or tragic event.

> The volunteer postventionist will participate in a debriefing session with Network team members and school officials.

> The volunteer postventionist shall facilitate small group discussions to educate students, parents and staff in areas such as suicide prevention, the grieving process and stress management.

I understand that I will not engage in any type of professional psychological counseling.

_____   _____

SIGNATURE   **DATE**

Sample Announcement to Faculty

Our student _____ died last night of an apparent suicide.

At this time, the investigation is still continuing and funeral arrangements are incomplete.

As we all knew _____, it is natural that both faculty and students will need to deal with some very intense feelings. A death by suicide is not easy for any of us.

The postvention support mechanism is in our building and will be available to talk with students and faculty to help us to cope with this loss.

If you would like to have a postvention team member talk to your class, please request this support.

Please announce this death to your 1st-hour class. All available information should be given in a calm, direct manner. Answer questions and allow as much time as needed to discuss feelings and reactions. If a student requests, or if you detect students who would benefit from joining the groups conducted by the postvention team, please allow them to do so.

Sample Announcement to Students

One of our students, _____, died last night. The death was an apparent suicide. The investigation is still continuing.

Since many of us knew _____, it is only natural that there will be some very deep feelings with which we will need to deal.

We are all sad, and we will need to help each other to talk about our loss and about our feelings.

Our counselors and our postvention team members are available to talk with anyone who would like to meet with them.

We will share information about the funeral when we receive it.

The family of _____ needs to know that we care, but they also need some privacy today.

Sample Comments to Media

The Youth Suicide Postvention Team is responding to our request to assist our students and faculty to cope with the shock and grief due to the apparent suicidal death of our student _____.

As we all knew _____, it is natural that both faculty and students will need to deal with some very intense feelings. A death by suicide is not easy for any of us.

The postvention support team will work with the counselors and faculty in our school to help students discuss their feelings and to help them cope with this loss.

If you want further information, please contact the principal of our building. Please do not attempt to interview students or faculty at this time. We all need some privacy now in order to deal with our grief.

Pre-Plan Format for Schools

Date _____

School _____

Principal _____ Phone _____

Postvention Team Contact _____

    Phone (home) _____ (work) _____

Alternate Postvention Contact _____

    Phone (home) _____ (work) _____

In-School Crisis Intervention Team Members
    Name   Home Phone

_____

_____

_____

_____

Attach documentation of plans for each individual school re:
    Usable rooms for groups
    Policies regarding student passes to and from class
    Other pertinent information

Bibliography

Allen, B. (1987, Summer). "Youth Suicide." *Adolescence* 22: 271–90.

Berg, B. (1982). *Teaching Students the True Meaning of "Dead Silence": A Curriculum for Teaching Students about Death.* Unpublished master's thesis, Sangamon State University, Springfield, Ill.

Bosworth, L. (1985, March). "Let's Call It Suicide." *Vanity Fair* 3:52–55, 108–10.

But, Jack Was a Good Driver (1974). Conflict and Awareness Film Series. DelMar, Calif.: Ziff-Davis Publishing Co. (CRM Films).

Cain, A. C. (1972). *Survivors of Suicide.* Springfield, Ill.: Charles C. Thomas.

Cantor, P. (1987). "Young People in Crisis: How You Can Help— A Guide for School Administrators, Faculty, Parents, Counselors, Clergy, Health Professionals, Social Workers, Friends." *The National Committee on Youth Suicide Prevention and American Association of Suicidology.*

Caplan, G. (1964). *Principles of Preventive Psychiatry.* New York: Basic Books.

Cantwell, D., and G. Carlson (eds.) (1983). *Affective Disorders in Childhood and Adolescence.* Jamaica, N.Y.: Spectrum Publications.

Carlson, G., and D. Cantwell (1982). "Suicidal Behavior and Depression in Children and Adolescents." *Journal of the American Academy of Child Psychiatry* 21:361–68.

Clark, C. (1987). "The Center for Suicide Research and Prevention." *Suicide Research Digest* 1:1:7.

Cohen-Sandler, R., A. Berman, and R. King (1982). "Lifestyles and Symptomatology: Determinants of Suicidal Behavior in Children." *Journal of the American Academy of Child Psychiatry* 21:178–86.

Coleman, J., J. Butcher, and R. Carson (1984). *Abnormal Psychology and Modern Life*. Glenview, Ill.: Scott, Foresman and Company.

Dempsey, R. A. (1986). *The Trauma of Adolescent Suicide: A Time for Special Leadership by Principals*. Reston, Va.: National Association of Secondary School Principals.

Den Houter, K. (1981). "To Silence One's Self: A Brief Analysis of the Literature on Adolescent Suicide." *Child Welfare* 15:2–9.

Doan, M., and S. Peterson (1984, November). "As 'Cluster Suicides' Take Toll of Teenagers." *U.S. News & World Report,* p. 12.

Dublin, L. (1963). *Suicide: A Sociological and Statistical Study*. New York: Ronald Press.

Elkind, D. (1985). "Teens in Crisis." *Focus on the Family* 4:2–4.

Friedrich, W., R. Reams, and J. Jacobs (1982). "Depression and Suicidal Ideation in Early Adolescents." *Journal of Youth and Adolescence* 11:403–7.

Giovacchini, P. (1981). *The Urge to Die*. New York: Macmillan.

Gispert, M., K. Wheeler, L. Marsh, and M. S. Davis (1985). "Suicidal Adolescents: Factors in Evaluation." *Adolescence* 20:80:753–62.

Glaser, K. (1981). "Psychopathologic Patterns in Depressed Adolescents." *American Journal of Psychotherapy* 35:368–82.

Gould, M., and D. Shaffer (1986, Sept. 11). "The Impact of Suicide in Television Movies: Evidence of Limitation." *New England Journal of Medicine* 315:690–94.

Greenberg, J. (1985, March). "Birth Trauma Linked to Adolescent Suicide." *Science News* 127:23, p. 183.

Grezegorek, A. (1979, September 19). *Suicide and Crisis Intervention*. Unpublished manuscript, Kent State University.

Grob, M., A. Klein, and S. Eisen (1983). "The Role of the High School Professional in Identifying and Managing Adolescent Suicidal Behavior." *Journal of Youth and Adolescence* 12:163–73.

Hals, E. (1985). "Suicide Prevention." *Health Education* 16:11:15–17.

Hamlin, W. T. (1982). "Adolescent Suicide." *Journal of the National Medical Association* 74:1:25–28.

Harkavy Friedman, J. M., G. M. Asnis, M. Boeck, and J. DiFiore (1987). "Prevalence of Specific Suicidal Behaviors in a High School Sample." *American Journal of Psychiatry* 144:9.

Hatton, C. L., and S. M. Valente (1981). "Bereavement Groups for Parents Who Survive a Suicidal Loss of a Child." *Suicide and Life Threatening Behavior* 11:141–50.

Hersh, J. (1985, January). "Interviewing College Students in Crisis." *Journal of Counseling and Development* 63:286–89.

Hunt, C. (1984). "Step By Step: How Your Schools Can Live Through the Tragedy of Teen Suicides." *American School Board Journal* 174:2:34–37.

Hicks, B. (1988). *Youth Suicide: Prevention-Intervention and Postvention Support.* Unpublished manuscript, University of Illinois, Urbana, Ill.

Hyde, M., and E. Forsyth (1978). *Suicide.* New York: Franklin Watts.

Johnson, W. (1985). "Classroom Discussion of Suicide: An Intervention Tool for the Teacher." *Contemporary Education* 56:2:114–17.

Klagsbrun, F. (1976). *Youth and Suicide.* Boston: Houghton Mifflin.

Kraft, D. (1980). "Student Suicides During a Twenty Year Period at a State University Campus." *Journal of the American College Health Association* 28:258–62.

Kreitman, N., P. Smith, and E. Tan (1970). "Attempted Suicide as Language: An Empirical Study." *British Journal of Psychiatry* 116:465–73.

Lazare, A. (1976). "The Psychiatric Examination in the Walk-In Clinic. *Archives of General Psychiatry* 33:96–102.

Lindemann, E. (1944). "Symptomatology and Management of Acute Grief." *American Journal of Psychiatry* 101:141–48.

Maag, J., and A. Meinhold (1985). "Review and Synthesis of Three Components for Identifying Depressed Students." *Monographs in Behavioral Disorders.*

Matter, D., and R. Matter (1984). "Suicide among Elementary School Children: A Serious Concern for Counselors." *Elementary School Guidance and Counseling* 18:260–67.

Mayo, D. J. (1984). "Confidentiality in Crisis Counseling: A Philosophical Perspective." *Suicide and Life Threatening Behavior* 14:2:96–112.

McGuire, D. (1984). "Childhood Suicide." *Child Welfare* 63:1: 17–26.

Miller, J. (1975). "Suicide and Adolescence." *Adolescence* 10: 13–23.

Miller, M. (1984). *Training Workshop Manual.* San Diego: Suicide Information Center (pp. 6–12).

Morgan, L. (1981). "The Counselor's Role in Suicide Prevention." *Personnel and Guidance Journal* 59:2–9.

National Center for Health Statistics (1978). *U.S. Vital Statistics 1974 and 1975 — Vol. II: Mortality.* Washington, D.C.

Nelson, F. L. (1981). "Suicide: Issues of Prevention, Intervention, and Facilitation." *Journal of Clinical Psychology* 10:8:1328–1333.

O'Carroll, P. (1987). *Recommendations to Help Communities Prevent "Cluster" Suicides.* Atlanta, Ga.: Centers for Disease Control.

Peck, M. (1982). "Youth Suicide." *Death Education* 6:29–47.

Pfeffer, C. (1986). *The Suicidal Child.* New York: Guilford.

———— (1987, January). "Reducing Environmental Stress for a Suicidal Ten-Year-Old." *Hospital and Community Psychiatry* 38:1:22–24.

Phillips, D. (1984). "Teenage and Adult Fluctuations in Suicide and Auto Fatalities." In *Suicide in the Young* ed. H. S. Sudak, A. B. Ford, and N. B. Rushforth (Boston: John Wright PSG, Inc.), p. 52.

Ray, L., and N. Johnson (1983, November). "Adolescent Suicide." *The Personnel and Guidance Journal* 10:131–35.

Richman, J. (1977). "Family and Environmental Aspects of Suicide." In *Suicide and Bereavement* ed. B. Danto and A. H. Kutscher (New York: MISS Information Corporation), pp. 119–23.

Ring, J. (1984). "Teen Suicide: Prevention, Intervention Response." *Cosad and Four Winds Hospital Manual,* pp. 13–16.

Robbins, D., and R. A. Conroy (1983). "A Cluster of Suicide Attempts: Is Suicide Contagious?" *Journal of Adolescent Health Care* 3:253–55.

Ross, C. (1980). "Mobilizing Schools for Suicide Prevention." *Suicide and Life Threatening Behavior* 10:239–43.

————, and R. Lee (1980) (undated). "Suicide in Youth and What You Can Do About It — A Guide for School Personnel." Pamphlet by the *Suicide Prevention and Crisis Center of San Mateo County,* 1811 Trousdale Drive, Burlingame, Calif.

Sawicki, S. (1988, Spring). "Effective Crisis Intervention." *Adolescence* 23:89:83–88.

Shaffer, D. (1974). "Suicide in Childhood and Early Adolescence." *Journal of Child Psychological Psychiatry* 15:275–91.

———— (1987, November–December). "Strategies for Prevention of Youth Suicide." *Public Health Reports* 102:60:611–13.

Shneidman, E. S. (1985, August). *Ten Commonalities of Suicide and Some Implications for Public Policy.* Paper presented at the Annual Convention of the American Psychological Association, Los Angeles, Calif.

———— (1987). "At the Point of No Return." *Psychology Today* 3:55–58.

Smith, D. (1976). "Adolescent Suicide: A Problem for Teachers." *Phi Delta Kappan* 57:539–42.

Stevenson, R. G., and H. L. Powers (1987). "How to Handle Death in the School." *Tips for Principals.* National Association of Secondary School Principals.

Topol, P., and M. Reznikoff (1982). "Perceived Peer and Family Relationships, Hopelessness and Locus of Control as Factors in Adolescent Suicide Attempts." *Suicide and Life Threatening Behavior* 12:141–50.

Valente, S. M., and J. R. Sellers (1986). "Helping Adolescent Survivors of Suicide." In *Adolescence and Death* ed. C. A. Corr and J. N. McNeil (New York: Springer).

Vidal, J. A. (1986). "Establishing a Suicide Prevention Program." *National Association of Secondary School Principals Bulletin* 70:192:68–71.

Waltzer, H. (1980). "Malpractice Liability in a Patient's Suicide." *American Journal of Psychotherapy* 34:1:89–98.

Weissman, M., B. Prusoff, G. Gammon, et al. (1984). "Psychopathology in the Children (Ages 6–18) of Depressed and Normal Parents." *Journal of American Child Psychiatry* 23:78–84.

Wright, L. (1982). "Parental Permission to Date and Its Relationship to Drug Use and Suicide Thoughts among Adolescents." *Adolescence* 17:409–418.

About *Youth Suicide:*
A Comprehensive Manual for Prevention and Intervention
and the National Educational Service

The mission of the National Educational Service is to help create environments in which **all** children and youth will succeed. *Youth Suicide: A Comprehensive Manual for Prevention and Intervention* is just one of many resources and staff development opporutnities we provide that focus on building a **Community Circle of Caring™**. If you have any questions, comments, articles, manuscripts, or youth art you would like us to consider for publication, please contact us at the address below.

Staff Development Opportunities Include:

Discipline with Dignity
Managing Disruptive Behavior
Ensuring Safe Schools
Improving Schools through Quality Leadership
Integrating Technology Effectively
Creating Professional Learning Communities
Building Cultural Bridges
Reclaiming Youth At Risk
Working with Today's Families

National Educational Service
1252 Loesch Road
Bloomington, IN 47404
(812) 336-7700
(888) 763-9045 (toll free)
FAX (812) 336-7790
e-mail: nes@nesonline.com
www.nesonline.com

NEED MORE COPIES OR ADDITIONAL RESOURCES ON THIS TOPIC?

Need more copies of this book? Want your own copy? Need additional resources on this topic? If so, you can order additional materials by using this form or by calling us at (888) 763-9045 or (812) 336-7700. Or you can order by FAX at (812) 336-7790.

Preview any resource for 30 days without obligation. If you are not completely satisfied, simply return it within 30 days of receiving it and owe nothing.

Title	Price*	Quantity	Total
Youth Suicide: A Comprehensive Manual for Prevention and Intervention	$ 19.95		
Reconnecting Youth: A Peer Group Approach to Building Life Skills	139.00		
Anger Management for Youth: Stemming Aggression and Violence	22.95		
Discipline with Dignity (3-video set and Comprehensive Guide)	445.00		
As Tough As Neccesary (4-video set and Comprehensive Guide)	495.00		
What Do I Do When...? How to Achieve Discipline with Dignity	21.95		
Rediscovering Hope: Our Greatest Teaching Strategy	19.95		
How to Create Safe Schools (3-video set and Leader's Guide)	295.00		
Safe Schools: A Handbook for Violence Prevention	25.00		
Breaking the Cycle of Violence (2-video set and Leader's Guide)	325.00		
Containing Crisis: A Guide for Managing School Emergencies	19.95		
Dealing with Youth Violence: What Schools and Communities Need to Know	18.95		
Teaching Self-Control	25.00		
Shipping & Handling: Please add 7% of order total, or a minimum of $3.00, if check or credit card information is not enclosed.			

*Price subject to change without notice.   TOTAL _____

❏ Check enclosed   ❏ Please bill me (P.O. #_____)
❏ Money Order   ❏ VISA, MasterCard, Discover, or American Express

Credit Card No._____ Exp. Date_____
Cardholder Signature _____

SHIP TO:
Name_____ Title _____
Organization _____
Address_____
City_____ State_____ ZIP _____
Phone_____ FAX _____

National Educational Service
1252 Loesch Road
Bloomington, IN 47404
(812) 336-7700 • (888) 763-9045 (toll free)
FAX (812) 336-7790
e-mail: nes@nesonline.com • www.nesonline.com

Do you have an idea to share?

We are always looking for quality manuscripts and video ideas that will be of benefit to others in the field. If you or one of your colleagues have a new, innovative, or effective approach to addressing timely issues, curriculum development, educator professionalism, or teaching, let us know. We'd like to hear from you. Contact:

Nancy Shin
Director of Publications